Praise for *Angel in the Rubble*

"I simply devoured *Angel in the Rubble*. I read it from cover to cover and found it impossible to put down! Genelle's hope was a choice that not only kept her alive for twenty-seven harrowing hours, but caused her to live her life in the aftermath of tragedy with deep conviction and passion. It is hard to read *Angel in the Rubble* without searching your own soul and asking yourself what truly matters. You will never look at your life, your family, or God the same again. This book is sure to impact the world, but more important, it will touch your heart in a profound way."

—Crystal Woodman Miller, survivor of the 1999 Columbine High School shooting and author of *Marked for Life*

"*Angel in the Rubble* is a riveting, simply-told story of strength, hope, and miracles by a simple, yet extraordinary, woman. It strengthened my faith in God, humanity, and those American values that make the USA the remarkable country it is. It's a potent shot of hope, whether Jew or Gentile, Muslim or Atheist."

—Wendy Fitzwilliam, Miss Trinidad & Tobago, author, and Miss Universe 1998

"Inspiring. Gripping. Riveting. Read this book. It will clasp you by the hand and compel you to get right with God and others—today. You'll be challenged to believe in miracles . . . in angels . . . in redemption . . . and most of all—in God Almighty."

—Robert Rogers, author of *Into the Deep: One Man's Story of How Tragedy Took His Family but Could Not Take His Faith* and founder of Mighty in the Land Ministry

ANGEL IN THE RUBBLE

The Miraculous Rescue of 9/11's Last Survivor

Genelle Guzman-McMillan

with William Croyle

HOWARD BOOKS
A DIVISION OF SIMON & SCHUSTER, INC.

NEW YORK   NASHVILLE   LONDON   TORONTO   SYDNEY   NEW DELHI

Howard Books
A Division of Simon & Schuster, Inc.
1230 Avenue of the Americas
New York, NY 10020

First Howard Books hardcover edition August 2011

HOWARD and colophon are trademarks of Simon & Schuster, Inc.

For information about special discounts for bulk purchases, please contact Simon & Schuster Special Sales at 1-866-506-1949 or business@simonandschuster.com.

The Simon & Schuster Speakers Bureau can bring authors to your live event. For more information or to book an event, contact the Simon & Schuster Speakers Bureau at 1-866-248-3049 or visit our website at www.simonspeakers.com.

Designed by Kyoko Watanabe

Manufactured in the United States of America

10 9 8 7 6 5 4 3 2 1

Library of Congress Cataloging-in-Publication Data

Guzman-McMillan, Genelle.
    Angel in the rubble / Genelle Guzman-McMillan.
        p. cm.
1. Guzman-McMillan, Genelle. 2. September 11 Terrorist Attacks, 2001—Biography. 3. Victims of terrorism—New York (State)—New York—Biography. 4. World Trade Center (New York, N.Y.)—Biography. I. Title.
    HV6432.7.G89 2011
    974.7'1044092—dc23
    [B]
                                                                          2011016814
ISBN 978-1-4516-3520-1
ISBN 978-1-4516-3521-8 (ebook)

To my husband, Roger, our four beautiful children, and all of my family and friends—this book would not have been possible without your eternal love and support.

To the families of the victims on September 11, 2001— your loved ones will never be forgotten. May you always feel the peace and comfort of God's warm embrace.

And to the dedicated heroes who selflessly and unconditionally gave your time, talents, and treasures to those of us who needed you—we will forever be indebted to you for your sacrifices.

ANGEL IN THE RUBBLE

PROLOGUE

I was the last survivor found beneath the World Trade Center rubble after the terrorist attacks on September 11, 2001. I was freed twenty-seven hours after the North Tower fell on me.

Though several other people were rescued from the devastation, we live in a world where numbers and placement are significant. Being the first, the one hundredth, the one thousandth, the one millionth, the last—they always seem to mean something to people. Having the moniker "The Last Survivor" has always been bittersweet for me.

Every time I hear those words, they are a stark reminder that nobody after me was found alive. The courageous rescuers—firefighters, police officers, and everyday citizens from New York City, across the country, and around the world—worked tirelessly for days to find as many survivors as they could, always hoping for one more. Just one more.

But somebody had to be the last.

To be found after so long was truly miraculous, the result of the effort and self-sacrifice of countless strangers with a goodness in their hearts far superior to the evil acts that prompted them to respond. I will forever be grateful for the second chance at life they gave me. Because of them, and because of the grace of God, I have the opportunity to share my story with the world today, a story I pray will bring hope to those who need it most.

CHAPTER ONE

September 11, 2001

I gently opened my eyes, reached over to the alarm clock, and tapped the snooze button a few minutes before six. It was still pitch-dark outside my east Brooklyn apartment, but daybreak was steadily advancing, about a half hour away.

As a smile formed on my face, I stretched my arms above my head and kicked the covers off. I was feeling invigorated that day. I'd had an especially deep, peaceful night's sleep.

It was a crisp, clear morning with a cool breeze filtering through the screen of my open bedroom window. The forecast was calling for a gorgeous, late-summer, eighty-degree day; my plans for a long-anticipated October vacation with a coworker to Miami, Florida, were going to be nailed down during my lunch hour; and my boyfriend, Roger, and I, were once again a happy couple. A bitter argument two weeks earlier nearly destroyed our relationship, but we had reconciled over the weekend. We were excited. Our reconciliation hadn't just salvaged our six-month romance; it had breathed a renewed passion into it. We felt more confident than ever that we were meant to be together.

On the morning of September 11, 2001, I had nothing in the world to be unhappy about. Life was good. Really good.

I took a short but warm and relaxing shower, then quickly brushed my teeth and combed through my closet for a cute outfit. My blissful mood dictated my attire as I slipped on a lilac blouse, my favorite black skirt, and two-inch high-heeled shoes. Since my days as a child on the Caribbean island of Trinidad, I loved to dress up. It didn't matter if I was going to church or playing outside with friends—taking care of my appearance was always important to me.

After applying the finishing touches on my makeup and hair, I took a deep breath and paused for a few seconds in front of the mirror to validate that I looked as good as I felt: beautiful, confident, energized. I smiled. Yep, I was ready. I clasped my watch on my left wrist, flipped off the bathroom light, and hurried into the kitchen to snag my keys, purse, and sunglasses off the table. I pressed the glasses firmly against my face and bolted out the front door, swiftly making the short jaunt through the radiant sunshine down Fulton Street and arriving at the train station in the nick of time to board the 7 a.m. train into Manhattan.

Overall, it was a pretty typical Tuesday morning. The only thing out of the ordinary was that Roger, who normally rode with me, was already in the city, having left much earlier than I to get a jump on some extra work he had at the office. Other than that, it was the usual, uneventful ride with the same unassuming strangers who accompanied me each day. The train made its two usual stops—at Chambers Street and at Broadway-Nassau where I got off at about 7:50 a.m. It was roughly a block away from the World Trade Center, a seven-building complex in Lower Manhattan. I worked at the Port Authority of New York and New Jersey on the sixty-fourth floor of the 110-story North Tower, also known as One World Trade Center or Tower One. It was one of those skyscrapers so colossal that it made you dizzy if you stood outside it and looked straight up. I had to take two of its dozens of elevators just to get to my floor.

I exited the elevator into the lobby on the sixty-fourth floor, walked through one of the four glass-door entrances to the office area, and headed for my desk. When I got there, I dropped my purse onto the chair and glanced at my watch: 8:05 a.m. Ugh! Five minutes late, and I still hadn't logged in for the day. I hustled as fast as my not-made-for-running stilettos would carry me to the other end of the floor, carefully weaving in and out of people along the way, to sign in.

The Port Authority, around since 1921, manages a lot of the infrastructure in the area that pertains to transportation, such as bridges, shipping ports, bus terminals, and airports. Its mission, simply put, is "To keep the region moving." I'd guess about seventy to eighty of the company's more than one thousand employees who were based in the World Trade Center worked on my floor, including top managers, architects, and engineers. I was an administrative assistant through a temporary-employment agency and had been working for the Port Authority since the beginning of the year. Though secretarial work through a temp agency may not sound the least bit glamorous, I took tremendous pride in every aspect of my job—typing important documents, setting up high-level meetings, answering the phone, running errands, simultaneously working for two bosses. My desk was in one of the dozens of drab, gray, high-partitioned cubicles in the middle of the expansive floor. It wasn't much to look at outside of the personal stamp I put on it with family photos—including a picture of my daughter, Kimberly—and a couple of small green plants, but it served its purpose. The management-level employees occupied the plush, private offices around the perimeter of the floor, which featured extravagant picture windows with spectacular views of the city.

After signing in, I made the trek back to my cube and booted up my computer. Knowing that was going to take a couple of minutes, I hopped on an elevator again, this time for a brief ride down to the forty-fourth-floor cafeteria. Though on a natural high that would have easily carried me through most of the day, my stomach was impatiently growling at me for its daily cream-cheese bagel and hot chocolate. I smiled and quickly said hello to a few coworkers I passed who were down there eating, but I didn't have time to hang around and socialize.

I got back to my desk and was able to take one small bite of my bagel and a tiny slurp of hot chocolate—the makeups of my daily breakfast—when the rat race suddenly, but predictably, shifted into high gear. Multiple phone lines lit up like a Christmas tree. A pile of mail, thicker than my bagel, was tossed on my desk for me to sort. I had a letter to draft that one of my bosses left behind the night before. It was an efficient system, and I rarely experienced time during the day with nothing to do. Keeping busy like that was something I enjoyed about my job . . . that, and the people I worked with.

At about 8:35, Susan Miszkowicz strolled over my way. Susan was a civil engineer who worked a couple of cubes down from mine and had become a great friend since I'd been there. She was in her late thirties, single, and lived with her mother in Brooklyn. She was generally a pretty quiet person with stunning blue eyes and a gorgeous, short hairstyle that I had always envied. She was also a leader in her profession, having belonged to the Society of Women Engineers and serving at one time as the president of the organization's New York Section. Susan was a very nice, intelligent and beautiful woman.

She asked how I was doing as she made herself at home next to me, casually leaning back against my desk, half sitting, half standing, and holding a large mug of steaming coffee with both hands as if it might try to escape. She had stopped by to relieve a little early-morning stress by venting a little about her boss. It was nothing spiteful, just the conventional frustrations we all have now and again with those we work for. She knew I was busy, but just like she was always there to lend an ear when I needed her, I was there to listen to her. And anyway, after eight months of working at the Port Authority, I had become pretty good at multitasking. A friendly chat, phone calls to answer, a letter to type, mail to sort, a bagel to eat . . . no problem.

Susan talked between sips of coffee. The more she vented, the more lighthearted she became. We chatted for about ten minutes, and she was getting ready to head back to her desk when her voice stopped cold in midsentence. My fingers, which had been idly typing my boss's letter, froze in sync with her sudden silence. My desk phone rang, but it became background noise as I was sucked in by a startling sound in the distance. I let the phone go to voice mail.

"Did you hear that?" Susan said.

"Yeah, I heard it."

It was a fleeting but strong noise that sounded eerily familiar, but I couldn't quite put my finger on it. I'd never heard a live gunshot before—only on television or in the movies—though I was pretty sure that was not it. It was more like smashing glass. That's what it was—a shattering sound. But the entire exterior of our building had glass windows. It could have been above us, below us, or maybe it wasn't in our building at all. It could have been an explosion in one of the other buildings in the complex. The South Tower, the twin to our tower, was right next door. Susan looked at me with the same clueless expression that I'm sure I had on my face.

"What was . . . ?"

Those are the only two words Susan could muster before she was abruptly silenced again, this time by a firm, steady vibration that rumbled beneath the floor, across the ceiling, and through the walls, shooting through like a perfectly pulsating drone, from one end of the room to the other.

Boomboomboomboomboomboomboomboomboom . . .

I instinctively snared the edge of my desk with both hands, thumbs on top and fingers underneath, as I forcefully pressed the soles of my shoes against the vibrating floor to brace myself. Susan slid her coffee cup onto my desk and hugged a wall of my cubicle. I heard several short screams and gasps from coworkers. Many more may have been drowned out by the noise. Everything and everyone shook violently and uncontrollably, enough that we were jolted an inch or two into the air. It rolled through just once, like a massive, single wave. But that was only the beginning of the chaos.

The moment the reverberating stopped, the entire building seemed to sway from top to bottom.

"Oh God!" Susan cried out, her voice trembling with fear and arms still tightly wrapped around the wall. One hundred ten floors of rugged steel and solid concrete, with thousands of human lives in its bosom, gently rocked . . . baaaack and forth . . . baaaack and forth . . . like a tree in a light wind. It wasn't strong enough to toss us around or knock us off our feet, but it was enough to terrify us. More screams and cries of distress echoed throughout the office.

That entire sequence of events—from the shattering noise to the rumbling to the final sway—lasted fifteen, maybe twenty, seconds. It was that quick, though it felt much, much longer. After the building stopped rocking and returned to its stable, upright position, I cautiously stood up. Still holding on to the desk with one hand just in case there were more chilling surprises to come, I fretfully gazed around the room. Mystified faces slowly emerged over several of the cubicle walls. Nobody appeared hurt. Nothing had toppled over that I could see. But that didn't stop some people from instinctively gathering their belongings and heading straight for the exits. It wasn't a mad rush. People seemed relatively calm. More than anything else, there were just a lot of bewildered looks darting around the room, accompanied by steady murmurs, as people speculated about what might have just happened.

What began for me as an especially happy day didn't feel so auspicious anymore. Skyscrapers were not supposed to move.

CHAPTER TWO

Stay or Go?

During the roughly twenty-eight years that I lived in Trinidad, I had survived a few harrowing earthquakes. There's nothing fun about them. You cannot prepare for them, since the rumbling and shaking begin without any forewarning. You're basically at their mercy, seeking shelter if you can, hoping that they end sooner than later. Though I'd lived in New York for less than two years, I was fairly certain that seismic activity on the East Coast was rare. But what other logical explanation could there have been for what we'd just experienced? Everything we'd felt mimicked what I'd lived through during earthquakes in Trinidad. And while I'd never been in a high-rise during an earthquake back home, it seemed pretty rational that the swaying of something so tall and freestanding might be a reasonable aftereffect.

Susan and I gingerly walked across the aisle to my boss's empty office to see if we could spot anything out of the ordinary happening outside. And we did. Floating through the air on the other side of the window were hundreds of pieces of paper and other debris. When you're that high up, anything that disrupts the view—other than maybe a plane or bird—is unusual. I fixated on the papers as they drifted down just inches from our faces, wishing I could make them freeze in midair long enough for me to read them and get an idea of where they were coming from. My eyes followed one piece as far down as they could, mesmerized at the extraordinary sight. It was gradually swinging back and forth and seemed to be descending much more slowly than the others. I tried to read it but couldn't make out what it was, and then I was distracted by something on the ground.

"Hey Susan, is that a fire down there?"

"Where?" She stood on her toes and strained her eyes, trying to see sixty-four floors below. It looked like flickering and alternating shades of orange and black, like flames and smoke.

Whether it was a fire or not, the papers falling from above made it unlikely that we were dealing with an earthquake. A window must have been broken, and I figured it would have been strange for an earthquake to cause a high-level, heavily paned window to break.

"A window had to have blown out," I said.

"That would at least explain the noise we heard," Susan added.

We pressed the sides of our faces against the glass and looked up as high and as close to the side of the building as we could. More paper, and lots of it, was pouring down from the clear blue sky. Had there been a gas explosion on one of the floors? Did the building even house gas? I knew nothing about the mechanics of it.

Frustrated that we hadn't learned anything new, Susan and I walked out into the main office to see if we could get a different view that would give us some better clues. Several people in other offices, doing the exact same thing we had been doing, were pulling their cheeks off the windows and turning away just as baffled. We roamed around the floor from one office to the next. About ten minutes had passed since the initial noise, when we bumped into Rosa Gonzalez.

Rosa sat five cubes down from me and had become a very good friend in my short time at the Port Authority. She was the one I was planning the trip to Miami with the following month. We had a lot in common: we were both secretaries and about the same age, neither of us was married, we each had a daughter from a previous relationship, and we both enjoyed occasionally hitting some of the area's nightclubs. We had never been to the clubs together, though. We had talked about joining up, but our schedules always seemed to conflict, so our social time had been relegated to lunch or coffee breaks at work. That was a big reason why we were so looking forward to our vacation together.

Her voice was even-keeled, but she looked nervous, even a little pale.

"I think a plane hit the building," she said softly. I wasn't sure that I heard her right.

"A plane? You're kidding." But she wasn't smiling. Of all the explanations . . . "Why do you think that?" I asked.

"That's just what I heard some other people saying," she said, gazing out the window.

"It's amazing how fast rumors can get going and take on a life of their own." I laughed nervously, trying to ease some of the tension. But Rosa just gave me a solemn look, as if she was certain that something terrible had happened.

At just about that moment, a supervisor named Joe Roque came by and said we needed to get out of the building. He was very short on details, but his tone was urgent. Despite his urgency, Rosa, Susan, and I did not jump at his words. Somehow, I just wasn't convinced yet that this was a full-scale emergency. It had been a good fifteen minutes or so since the building had swayed. Why panic now when things seemed stable? And anyway, the thought of rushing down to the ground floor with thousands of people, either by crowded elevators or, worse, down the stairs, was not very inviting. I felt like I needed more information. In light of Rosa's bleak demeanor, I was surprised that she didn't turn to leave immediately. At the time, I was glad. I felt that she, Susan, and I needed to stick together.

Some people on the floor didn't hesitate to follow Joe's instructions and instantly headed for the elevators or stairs. I think many of them were longtime employees who were working in the North Tower back in 1993 when a truck full of explosives was planted and detonated in the parking garage underneath, killing six people and heavily damaging some of the lower floors. I guess if I had been around when that bomb was set off, I probably would have felt more compelled to bail too.

I also realized that I hadn't heard a siren or public-address announcement signaling anyone to evacuate. That was the protocol I'd been taught since I started working there. I'd gone through a few disaster and fire drills, and the first signs that there was an

14

emergency were always the same—the siren, followed by an announcement. I scanned the floor and saw and heard nothing that
suggested to me that we should leave. From what I could see, the
power was still on. There was no smoke. No fire. My gut told me
the worst was over.

Soon enough, Rosa, Susan, and I went back to our respective
desks to make some phone calls. I dialed Roger. He worked nearby
as a press operator at American Direct Mail and had a good view
of our building. I thought maybe he could see something more
informative from where he was.

"Hi honey," I casually said when he answered.

"Hey, what's up?"

"Well, I'm not exactly sure. Something happened here at
work, but we don't know what."

"What do you mean 'something happened'?"

"I don't know. We heard some sort of crashing noise and felt
the building shake. It was very weird. I think it's above us because
there was a bunch of paper falling down outside. Some people
think a plane might have hit us—"

"A plane?" he interrupted.

"Yeah. One guy suggested that we evacuate, but there aren't
any sirens or anything, so we're just not sure. I'm a little nervous
about leaving the building with a potential stampede of others.
Can you see anything unusual over here from where you're at?"

He said he hadn't heard anybody at his office talking about
it—which, in retrospect, is surprising, but it also demonstrates the
utter suddenness of the attack—so he told me to hang on while he
walked over to a window with a view of our building.

"Wow, there's a lot of smoke coming from near the top."

"Smoke?"

"I can't really tell what floors, but it's above you," he said. "I guess it's possible that a plane could have hit, but I don't see anything sticking out anywhere."

"What do you think I should do?"

Roger took a deep breath. "I think it's probably safest to leave now. It's going to be chaotic either way, and you're better safe than sorry."

"You're probably right."

"I'll leave here now too," he said. "I'll meet you at Century 21 in about twenty minutes." Century 21 Department Store, a popular wholesale clothing store in Manhattan, was across the street from my building and was the usual meeting spot for us any time he came over.

"Okay," I said. "Sounds good. I love you."

"I love you too."

I hung up the phone and took a deep breath, feeling a sense of relief that everything was going to be okay—but I also started to wonder just how bad it was above me. How much smoke was "a lot"? Could a small plane really have caused it? Had the people up there been evacuated before the event—whatever it was? If not, was everybody up there okay?

Since it would only take me a couple of minutes to ride the elevator to the ground floor—even if the ride was accompanied by lots of people—I took one last walk around the area just to see what other people were doing and saying. Almost everyone was on the phone. It sounded like a few were speaking with their significant others. I heard at least one person talking to what I think was a 911 operator. Another, I'm pretty sure, was talking to the Port

Authority police. But the one common theme I noticed was that after they hung up the phone, they grabbed their coats and headed calmly for the exits.

I went back to my cube and clicked a couple of buttons on my computer to save the letter I'd been typing before closing it out. I could finish it tomorrow. I grabbed my purse and went over to Susan's desk, but she was gone. Her computer was on and her purse was there, so I assumed she was still somewhere on the floor. I wanted to find her to see if she wanted to go down with me. I continued first, though, toward Rosa's desk, figuring she would probably want to leave too. When I got to her desk, she was there—but hunched over in her chair with her face buried in her hands.

"Rosa?" She looked up at me with tears in her eyes. The Rosa I knew had always been happy and fun with a great sense of humor and never seemed to let too much bother her. I had never seen her this way before.

"What happened? Are you okay?" I asked her, reaching out and touching her shoulder.

Her voice quivered.

"Genelle," she said. She looked overwhelmed by fear. "We need to get out of here."

CHAPTER THREE

Terrorism

I've always seen myself as a mentally tough person. I had to be strong when I was younger because I grew up in a household with nine siblings, where there were always spirited battles for space and attention. My siblings and I got along pretty well, but sometimes I had to fight for what I wanted and stand up for myself. Sure, I could be soft and emotional too, but I rarely faced a situation I didn't feel capable of handling on my own. That day, however, tested my grit.

"Rosa, what's wrong? Why are you crying?" Seeing those tears and that fear in her eyes sent my heart racing. I felt a sudden shortness of breath.

"I'm scared," she said. "I just want to be with Jennifer right now."

Jennifer was her daughter who was in school that morning. She was roughly the same age as my daughter, Kimberly, who was twelve. I had never met Jennifer, but I felt like I knew her because of how much Rosa talked about her. She was Rosa's pride and joy. I knew the feeling.

It became obvious, by Rosa's emotional state, that she had quite a different reaction than I to our present situation. I knew we needed to get out of the building. But I got the sense from Rosa that she believed death was knocking on our door, that we might never get out, and that she may never see her daughter again. Was she right?

I began to focus my thoughts on Kimberly, my own pride and joy, and how much I missed her. Kimberly was living in Trinidad with her father, Elvis. We had her when I was just eighteen. Though we never married, Elvis and I lived together for six years in a quiet home in the country before we broke up. We were good parents when we were together. He was the breadwinner of the family while I was a stay-at-home mom during Kimberly's early years. I was up with her through the nights and took care of her each day. When Elvis came home from work, he would give me a break by making dinner and taking care of her. We took her to church every Sunday and provided her with everything she needed. It was a good team effort. Even after Elvis and I separated, we had an amicable relationship and continued to make Kimberly our focus.

But I left my baby in 2000 for New York to pursue my dream of singing and dancing professionally. I planned to bring her to live with me as soon as I was established and closer to that dream. Until then, we shared only a couple of visits together a year. It had been more than a month since I'd seen her. Now I wondered if I'd ever see her again. Or Roger, for that matter. Or any of my family. My heart sank.

My thoughts grew darker as more grim news rolled in. I overheard some people talking about black smoke that was seeping in through a couple of our floor's glass doors. Several people gathered some coats, soaked them in water in the kitchen sink, and set them down at the base of the doors. They also sealed the door frames with tape to try and keep the smoke at bay. Pat Hoey and Pasquale Buzzelli, two managers on the floor, joined in the efforts by hustling to another glass door that someone must have inadvertently left open when leaving the building, which had allowed the smoke to roll in more swiftly. They shut the door, tossed down some wet coats, and taped it up. I don't know how long it took everybody to do all that, but it seemed like just a minute or two. Rosa was still sitting in her chair, regaining some composure, seemingly unaware of the commotion caused by the smoke—and I wanted to keep it that way. I was struggling to keep my emotions in check, watching all of this, but there was no need to upset her any more than she already was. She seemed to know better than anyone just how catastrophic this was.

"Rosa, we're going to be fine," I said, unsure of whether I was telling the truth. "But you're right, let's just get out of here."

What I really needed at that moment was a time-out. Just a two-minute stoppage of the world. Long enough for me to find Susan and for the three of us to start making our way out of the building. Nothing else to distract us. Nothing else to shift our thinking in another direction. Nothing else to make us question whether or not we should leave. But life doesn't work that way.

During those next couple of minutes, everything grew even more intense.

Pat Hoey had retreated into his office and was on the phone, not too far from Rosa and me. He was speaking to a Port Authority police sergeant, who was giving Pat instructions:

PAT: "Sergeant, this is Pat Hoey. I'm with the Port Authority. I'm in the Trade Center."

SERGEANT: "What's up?"

PAT: "I'm on the sixty-fourth floor."

SERGEANT: "Okay."

PAT: "In Tower One."

SERGEANT: "Alright."

PAT: "I've got about twenty people here with me."

SERGEANT: "Okay."

PAT: "What do you suggest? Staying tight?"

SERGEANT: "Stand tight. Is there a fire right there where you are?"

PAT: "No. There is a little bit of smoke on the floor."

SERGEANT: "It looks like there is an explosion in (Tower) Two."

PAT: "Okay . . ."

SERGEANT: "So be careful. Stay near the stairwells and wait for the police to come up."

PAT: "They will come up, huh? Okay. They will check each floor? If you would, just report that we're up here."

SERGEANT: "I got you."

PAT: "And I'm on . . . if you need the number, it's 5397."

SERGEANT: "I got you."

PAT: "Thank you."
SERGEANT: "Alright, bye."

While a defined path was what we had been looking for from the start, getting the sergeant's directive completely altered our thinking and likely changed our future forever. Pat hung up the phone and came out of his office.

"Listen up, everybody," he said with his hands cupped around his mouth, trying to make sure everyone heard him. "They told us not to leave. They are sending police up, and we need to wait here. We're going to be fine."

My anxiety began to subside a bit. A few people around the room were even smiling and began casually chatting. Rosa wasn't as jovial, but she also wasn't crying anymore. Pat's words obviously made her feel better too. Not only were we told to stay put, but police were on their way up, which told me that the building had to be safe.

For roughly the next twenty to thirty minutes, my coworkers and I continued to comfort one another and reassure each other that we were going to be fine. Some of us speculated about what had happened—we were still in the dark—and some got back on the phone with friends and family. The one thing none of us was doing was working. We were far too distracted.

I stayed at Rosa's desk, and Susan joined us after a few minutes. Rosa and I talked about anything positive we could think of—Jennifer, Kimberly, our trip to Miami, maybe finally getting together one of these upcoming weekends. It seemed to be helping us—until we heard a hysterical scream.

"That's us! That's our building!" I didn't know who was shouting, but the sound came from the direction of the conference room. Susan dashed madly toward the voice. Rosa jumped up from her chair as we chased after Susan. Several other people converged on the room at the same time. There were a couple of people in there watching television, watching . . . us?

"Oh God!" Rosa shrieked before pressing her hand against her mouth. Within seconds her breathing became laborious. I put my arms around her, trying futilely to comfort us both.

Staring at the television, I couldn't believe what I saw. Thick, daunting, black clouds of smoke billowed from the top floors of our building. It was beyond surreal, one of those moments where every few seconds I had to keep reminding myself that what I was watching was real and not just a bad dream. That really was our building burning, and on live television!

Someone grabbed the remote and flipped channels. There we were again. *Click.* Again. *Click.* Again. We were all over the news, local and national. *Wow,* I thought. *What in the world is going on?*

"How far above us is the smoke?" I asked nobody in particular. No one answered. I tried to count down the floors, starting at the top from 110, but it was impossible. The windows appeared too small on the television screen, and there was too much smoke to be able to see them clearly enough.

I noticed that the South Tower next door to us was on fire too. Roger hadn't said anything about that. How could it be possible that both towers were burning? Did the plane that everyone had been talking about go through one and also smash into the other?

"Shhh. Shhh," someone said, trying to hear the television reporter above the chatter in the room. Everybody stopped talking and listened, but the news only confused us, or at least me, even more. The reporter said that the buildings were hit by separate planes, and that they were likely terrorist attacks.

I was stunned. To me, a terrorist attack on a building involved men in dark clothing or fatigues bursting through the doors with machine guns, scaling the outside of the building, or securing hostages. Hollywood movies played through my head. *Die Hard* came to mind. How in the world could a plane crash be a terrorist attack? It made no sense. Wouldn't the terrorists die too? What would they gain? Nothing made any sense at that point.

It was then, once I was able to see the devastation and hear the reporters say that two separate planes had hit the towers, when I realized that lives had been lost on the floors above us. People I possibly just saw in the cafeteria or rode the elevators with or even rode the train into work with. All they did was come to work, and just like that, they were gone. My body trembled at the reality of it all.

Suddenly desperate to escape, I reminded myself of the sergeant's instructions and that the only thing that had changed since those orders was our heightened awareness. But why was it safer to stay put? How could that be? It certainly didn't look safe to me. It didn't look safer to Roger when I talked to him. Oh my God—Roger! I'd completely forgotten that he told me to meet him outside twenty minutes after we hung up. Those twenty minutes were long gone. He must be worried sick.

Rosa and I decided to leave the conference room. We had seen enough. We walked hand in hand toward her desk, followed by the rest of the group. The group scattered in different directions, mainly to their desks. I think they all agreed that watching the news wasn't helping anybody. When we got to Rosa's cube, I

handed her a few tissues from a box on her desk. She was still trying to reestablish her breathing.

"I need to go make a phone call. I'll be right back, okay?"

"Okay," she said softly.

I did not own a cell phone and did not want to call Roger
from her desk phone in case our conversation were to upset her
even more.

I raced to my desk to call Roger on his cell.

Next to Kimberly, nobody ranked higher in my life than
Roger. He was also from Trinidad and was living in New York
when I moved there. We actually met, though, in our native
land in February 2001, during my second vacation back home
to visit Kimberly. It was at the annual carnival, an enormously
popular event in Trinidad and Tobago. (Tobago is a tiny island
next to Trinidad; together they form the Republic of Trinidad
and Tobago.) The carnival takes place the two days before Ash
Wednesday, similar to Mardi Gras in New Orleans. Roger and
his brother Bryan were at the carnival when Roger spotted me
from a distance.

There are more than a million people in Trinidad and Tobago,
and it seemed like Bryan knew just about all the women. It just so
happened that Bryan was one of Elvis's friends, so he already knew
me. He called me over to meet Roger and introduced me to him
as Judy, which was my given name at birth. Genelle was actually
my middle name but the name I preferred to be called. I was still
called Judy, though, by most people in Trinidad.

Roger and I hit it off immediately. He was tall and handsome
with an infectious smile and a wonderful sense of humor. We ex-
changed phone numbers and agreed to go out when we got back

to the States. He wasted no time calling me the following week, and our love just took off from there. In fact, we got along so un-believably well that I moved in with him just a few months later. I know that's quick, but I just had a feeling that he was the one, and he felt the same way about me.

But now . . . now what? I was getting more and more nervous about our situation in the building as I imagined never seeing Roger again either.

I dialed his cell, but his voice mail kicked on. I hung up and tried again. Still no answer. This time I left a message.

"Honey, I'm still inside the building," I said, trying to keep a steady voice. "I don't know. We have to wait until somebody comes and gets us out, okay? I'll try and call you back again. Bye. I love you."

I stood up and couldn't see or hear Rosa, so I assumed she was okay. I decided to take another minute to try and sneak in a call to Lauren, my cousin who lived in Queens. My sister, Christine, was visiting from Trinidad and was staying with her. My Aunt Gaily, Lauren's mom, was also there. I didn't want to call Kimberly, because I didn't want to alarm her. I knew she would be in school, and pulling her out of class with the news would only worry her.

"Hello?" the voice on the other end said. It was Lauren's.

"Lauren, it's Genelle."

"Oh my God, Genelle! Did you see what happened?" Neither she, nor anybody in my family, knew I worked at the World Trade Center. They knew I worked in Manhattan and that I was em-ployed as a temp for the Port Authority, but they had no idea what building I was in—something that just never came up in conversa-tion, I guess. Before the attacks that day, the World Trade Center was, in some ways, just another construction in Manhattan—a beautiful and iconic one, but to me, it was an office building. Simple as that.

Lauren was talking a mile a minute, giving me a play-by-play of what she was watching on television. My sister and aunt were in the background talking over each other. It sounded like there were twenty people in the room.

"Laur . . . Laur . . ." I tried to interrupt her, but she wouldn't stop talking. "LAUREN!" I finally got her to stop.

"What? What's wrong, Genelle?" she asked.

"Lauren, listen to me—I'm in that building on TV," I said louder than necessary. I was trying to keep a cool tone, but at this point I had very little calm in my reserves. My attempts at composure didn't soothe Lauren. She let out a scream that made me move the phone off my ear.

"Oh my God! Genelle's in there!" she cried. My sister and aunt screamed in unison.

"Lauren? Lauren?" I couldn't make out what anybody was saying, and she couldn't hear me. I was getting frustrated. Then suddenly, out of nowhere, I heard a thud. All the noise stopped for a couple seconds.

"What was that?" I asked as Lauren yelled over me halfway through my question.

"Oh no. Christine? Christine? Genelle, Christine fainted. Christine?"

Almost on cue with Christine's fainting, the building began to sway again.

CHAPTER FOUR

Mixed Messages

The second sway felt exactly like the first: an uncomfortable back-and-forth rocking, like the start of that pirate ship ride at amusement parks. It wasn't so forceful that it felt like the building was going to tip over or snap in half, but it was enough to make me question why I hadn't immediately left after the first time it happened. Screams rang out across the room from the one or two dozen people who remained. I was still on the phone, though I didn't know if Lauren was actually on the other end. I could hear voices, but I assumed she'd put the phone down since Christine was out cold.

With my shoulder holding the receiver to my ear, I clenched my teeth and latched onto the desk again, waiting patiently for the swaying to stop. It probably lasted about ten seconds . . . ten very long seconds.

"I love you guys!" I yelled to Lauren, unsure if she heard me. "I need to get out of here!" I hung up, and my heart started rapidly beating again. I grabbed my purse, took a quick look around my desk to make sure there was nothing else I needed, and darted over to Rosa's desk. She was still using the tissues and still breathing heavily.

"Rosa, just concentrate on each breath, okay? Concentrate on each breath."

But it's awfully difficult to focus on something and gain control of your emotions when bad news keeps steamrolling in. This time it was the smoke. It was getting thicker and thicker in the lobby and was finding every crevice available to force its way into our office. It still hadn't reached the area where Rosa and I were, but I could see it lurking on the other side of the room, slowly creeping toward us. Pasquale and another gentleman, Steve Fiorelli, knew, like the rest of us, that we were going to have to find a way out. They took it upon themselves to find the way. They removed the tape from the edges of one of the lobby doors, pushed their way through the smoke, and opened the door to one of the stairwells. They assumed it was going to be a no-go but were pleasantly surprised to find the stairwell relatively clear of smoke, very well lit, and empty. By that point, everybody who had chosen to leave the building was probably out, or close to it. It was sobering to be among the last to leave.

They came back into the office, near where Rosa and I were. Pasquale took charge, which was exactly what we needed.

"This is crazy. We have to get out of here now," he said, snapping us out of our confused stillness. Everybody stopped what he or she was doing and migrated toward him.

"The elevators aren't working," he said. "We'll have to take the stairs."

Not ideal, but it was our only option.

It was a little after 10 a.m. As Rosa stood up, I picked up her phone and tried to call Roger once more. Voice mail again. I didn't bother leaving another message. We needed to go. I took Rosa's hand, and we walked together toward Pasquale and the rest of the group, which included Susan. There were fifteen of us. Pat Hoey was the sixteenth. He was nearby in his office, making one last call to the Port Authority Police to tell them our plans:

PAT: "Hi, this is Pat Hoey. I'm in the Trade Center, Tower One. I'm with the Port Authority, and we are on the sixty-fourth floor. The smoke is getting kind of bad. So we are going to . . . we are contemplating going down the stairway. Does that make sense?"

POLICE DESK: "Yes. Try to get out."

PAT: "OK."

POLICE DESK: "OK?"

PAT: "Thank you."

POLICE DESK: "All right. Bye."

Pat came out of his office and told Pasquale that we were okay to go. A few people were wiping away tears, but everybody seemed collected and strong enough to leave.

"The stairwell looked pretty clear," Pasquale said. "Is everybody ready?"

"NO!" came a shout from the back of the group. What? Who was that? Was he kidding? I turned to see an older man. I didn't know him well but saw him often and knew he was an engineer on the floor. Did I really just hear him say no? Was this nightmare ever going to end?

"This building was designed so that it cannot fall," he said with a thick Russian accent. "It will sway, but it will not fall. We need to listen to what they told us and stay here."

The whole convoluted morning had been nothing but mixed messages. And, of course, no matter how tapped out we felt, we couldn't will the terrible events to stop. After the Russian man spoke, the power on one side of the floor went out.

I simply couldn't deal with it anymore and finally let myself cry. Rosa squeezed my hand tighter. I felt at that moment like I had let her down, like I should have stayed strong for her, but I also didn't want to be strong. I just wanted to be somewhere else. In Trinidad with Kimberly. Outside with Roger. Anywhere but here.

I thought about my mortality. What if this was it for me? What if I died here? That distinct possibility triggered thoughts of my faith, or lack of it. I was born and raised Catholic and went to church for about the first twenty-eight years of my life, either at a Catholic church with my parents or a Pentecostal church with Elvis. Once I got to New York, I didn't go to church at all. But for many of those years that I went in Trinidad, I was simply going through the motions to appease my parents or Elvis or to set a good example for Kimberly. I'd mentally drifted from God as I focused more on me and the material side of life. I believed in God, but not enough to acknowledge His everyday impact on my life. If I didn't make it out of the tower, what was in store for my soul? I was too scared to think about it.

"Genelle, don't worry," Susan said as if she had been reading my mind. She was trying to stay strong herself as she put her arms around me while Rosa and I continued to hold hands. "We will be all right."

Pasquale saw and felt our fear and visibly refused to second-guess himself. He overruled the Russian man on behalf of us all.

"That's it," he said decisively. "We're going now."

CHAPTER FIVE

Descent

We swiftly scurried as a cohesive group to the other side of the office, through the smoke in the lobby, and toward the stairwell door, passing the dormant elevators that I'd ridden just two hours earlier. It was exasperating to even look at them, knowing that if we could ride them, it would take us just a fraction of the time and energy that walking would. But we'd waited far too long and now had no choice.

We kept our heads down, covered our mouths and noses, and squinted our eyes as we muscled our way through the smoke. I heard a few random coughs, but, overall, it sounded like everybody was making it through okay. The smoke was thick, but we could see. I was still hand in hand with Rosa.

"You doing okay?" I asked her.

"Mmm-hmm" she said, nodding her head. "You?"

"I'm good," I lied. None of us was good, but we were trying to stay as positive as we could.

When we got to the steel door—the only thing that stood between the stairs and our hope for freedom—Pasquale paused for a brief moment and stood solemnly as if we were about to enter another dimension. I think most of us were a little nervous about what we would find on the other side of the door, even though Pasquale had told us it was clear. But that was a few minutes before when he and Steve checked. The way things were changing on a dime all morning, we didn't trust much.

Without further delay, Pasquale flung the door open. I was right behind him and nudged myself as close to him as I could.

It was just as he had said. Nothing. No fire. Hardly any smoke. The lights were on for as far as we could see. Finally, something had gone right. It was a minor victory, but a victory nonetheless. Pasquale had a flashlight he'd found in an emergency kit in a closet, but thankfully it looked like we wouldn't need it.

We had a long way to go—more than half the height of the building. The stairwell was like any solid, concrete stairwell in a skyscraper. You descended maybe ten steps or so, turned at the landing, then descended roughly another ten steps. That was one floor. It didn't sound too bad when broken down like that. But when doing the math—ten steps, plus ten steps, times sixty-four floors . . . I tried not to think about it.

While holding the door open, Pasquale turned and faced us and told everybody to line up single file. I was still second in line, right behind him. Pat and Steve were toward the back. Rosa was on my heels, holding my hand. Two people behind Rosa was

Susan, who was still pretty composed. In between Rosa and Susan was the Russian man. Despite his insistence that we not go and his assurance that the building would not fall, he was with us. I guess he figured there was no point in being left behind. I was relieved he came.

Our descent was orderly and we stayed close together, leaving no more than a step or two between each of us. We weren't zipping down but were moving at a pretty decent clip. I thought about carrying my shoes since going barefoot would have been less painful than wearing heels, but my hands were full. I already had my purse over one shoulder, one hand in Rosa's, and my other hand on the railing. For now, I'd leave the shoes on. There wasn't much chatter from anybody that I could hear, other than Pasquale periodically assuring us that everything ahead looked clear and asking us every few flights how we were doing.

"We're good. Keep going," was the general response. The overall mood of the group was pretty upbeat. And why not? We were finally on our way out.

The floors were clearly marked at each landing. As tired as we were quickly becoming, it seemed that around the fiftieth floor we were able to reenergize ourselves. I don't know why. I guess there's just something psychological about that number when you're in a roughly one-hundred-story building. Once we passed it and saw the forty-ninth floor, we felt like we were making progress and were closer to the end of our journey than the beginning, even though we'd only gone down fifteen floors. The next milestone came at about the forty-second floor, where, to our surprise, we found some New York City firemen in full gear sitting on the steps. Pasquale slowed down as we went by them.

"What are you guys doing here?" Pasquale asked.

"Just trying to catch our breaths," one of them said with sweat dripping from his forehead and a bottle of water in hand as he spoke between heavy gasps. I felt weary just looking at them with all of that heavy clothing and equipment hanging from their tired bodies. I'm not sure why they were going up or where their final destination was. Maybe it was our floor. Maybe higher. Going down was difficult enough. I couldn't imagine climbing up like they were.

"How is everything?" Pasquale asked.

"It's all good," another one said confidently as he stood up to prepare for the next leg of his climb. "You're fine. Just be careful going down."

I know firefighters perform dangerous jobs and save lives every day, but having never needed one before, I didn't realize until that moment what heroes they truly are. I admit I took them for granted. If something is on fire, you call them, they come and put it out, you say thank you, they leave, and that's it. If you're watching a fire on the news, your attention is usually captured by the spectacular flames and smoke, not the brave men and women fighting those flames and rescuing people. To actually see those men on the stairs with all that gear, walking all that way into danger instead of trying to escape, staggered my mind. How much braver can somebody be? Their mere presence gave me hope that we were going to make it.

"Did you hear what they said, Rosa?" I asked her with some enthusiasm as we continued on. "We're going to be fine." Those words were as much for me as they were for her.

We eagerly continued down. The lights, thank God, were still on. I took a quick look at my watch: it was about 10:20 a.m. when we got to the thirtieth floor. The single-file line was still pretty much intact. I looked over my shoulder and could tell the Russian man was struggling, getting very tired, but he was still keeping up and seemed determined not to fall behind. Susan and everyone following her seemed to be doing well. We got to the landing on about the twenty-fifth floor when Rosa suddenly stopped. I was surprised since she'd been staying right at my side and seemed to be doing well enough.

"Everything all right, Rosa?"

"Genelle," she said through deep breaths, "why don't you take off your shoes?"

There had been very little to smile about the past couple of hours, but that made me spontaneously laugh out loud. It wasn't just the comment, but the timing of it. We were all so stressed out, yet Rosa broke the tension, even if just for a brief moment, by taking stock of my footwear. It felt ironic and somehow meaningful at once. She was right, my feet were killing me. Clomping down on all those hard steps in those things was no picnic. I honestly don't know why I hadn't taken them off before, and I have no idea if other women in high heels were wearing their shoes or not. With all that was going on, I probably didn't have the brain space to even think about it.

"I need these shoes, Rosa," I said with a grin. "What am I going to wear when we get outside?" She cracked a smile, even chuckled a bit. We were in our own blissful world for those few seconds—another energy-boosting point on our journey.

"Keep moving!" came a terse shout from the back of the line. We continued down, picking up some steam. We passed the twentieth floor . . . nineteen . . . eighteen . . . seventeen . . .

sixteen. I watched Pasquale as he continued to lead the way and realized what a great debt I felt toward him for taking leadership. We needed a strong voice to take charge in what had become a chaotic situation. Had he not taken the initiative to escape, we would have probably still been sitting at our desks doing nothing but worrying. It's hard to explain how that makes sense. Why wouldn't we have just left on our own? Didn't the evidence convince us that we were not safe? But at the time, we were dumbstruck. There was too much confusion, and we were stunned to stillness.

I felt a similar admiration for Pat and Steve, who were anchoring the back of the line. Pat made the phone calls to the police. Steve helped Pasquale check out the stairs. I felt safe and confident as I recognized I was walking among heroes.

We hit the fifteenth floor . . . fourteen . . . thirteen. That's when I finally had to stop and take my shoes off. My feet were aching badly and couldn't take anymore.

"Hang on," I said to Rosa. "Let me take these things off."

"I told you," she said, grinning at me.

With her facing me, I put my right hand on her left shoulder and raised my left foot behind me to slide the shoe off. But I started to lose my balance. I looked at Rosa, who had one hand on the railing. Why was she also losing her balance? I began to tumble over. It wasn't just me, or her. Everything, everyone, was shaking. Susan, the rest of the people in line, the railing they were desperately clinging to. Everything above us, below us, next to us. It was similar to the earthquake-like feeling when all of this started, only a hundred times worse. Rosa slipped out of my grip to turn and run back up the stairs.

"Rosa!" I shouted. I don't have any idea if she heard me, and I don't know why she began to run upstairs. But it didn't matter in what direction anyone ran. The stairs above us were crumbling. The walls surrounding us burst open like a couple of semitrucks had smashed through them. The floor under our feet was cracking in every which way. I put my face down and covered my head with my arms as concrete chunks of every shape and size poured down from above and pelted my body, like I was being stoned to death. Huge clouds of dust rose from the ground and encircled me, burning my eyes and making it nearly impossible to breathe. With every passing second, the ferocious noise around me grew louder and louder, the shaking more and more violent.

There was no escape. I was helpless. We all were. I don't know how I withstood the physical beating, but the emotional pain of knowing that this was the end of my life and that I would never see Kimberly or Roger again was much worse. It was over. I cried out their names as I dropped hard to my knees while the North Tower of the World Trade Center fell on top of me.

CHAPTER SIX

Buried Alive

Brutal, diabolical, painful, vicious. Those are some of the words I've used to attempt to depict the hell of being hammered into the ground by more than ninety floors of a free-falling building. But no word will ever be sufficient.

I'd been in onerous situations before but never one that was 100 percent hopeless. That was the worst part about it—the hopeless feeling. No matter which direction I turned, I couldn't avoid it. There was no way to physically protect myself. There was no shelter I could hide under, because it was my shelter that had beaten me down. None of the people I was with could help, because they were living the same horror. It wasn't something that mental toughness could overcome. There was no escape.

What made it worse was that we had come so close to getting out. We had traveled down more than fifty floors, with only a handful to go, and were in the best spirits we had been in since the turmoil started. By the fifteenth floor, it didn't cross our minds that we would not make it. Even if the lights had gone out, we had Pasquale's flashlight. Even if someone had collapsed from exhaustion, we were close enough to the ground floor that a couple of us could have carried him or her. We never imagined at that juncture that anything could stop us.

The terror of the collapse lasted about thirty seconds, I would guess—probably not even that long. But it felt like an eternity. Unthinkable amounts of thick concrete, heavy steel, sharp glass, and God-only-knows-what-else pummeled every square inch of our bodies. It was not just the makeup of the building itself, but everything in it: hundreds, or even thousands, of desks, chairs, filing cabinets, bathrooms, pipes, air conditioners, elevators, and appliances, not to mention the airplane that started it all. And the people. Oh God . . . the people.

I could do absolutely nothing after falling to my knees but crouch into a fetal position. I laid there with my head buried in my arms, eyes squeezed shut, teeth clenched, and breath held as debris rained down. I was too tense to cry or scream. I had no choice but to succumb. Finally, after what felt like forever, the crashing stopped. When it did, my world shifted. It went from a white cloud of dust and whirlwind of pandemonium to total darkness and sheer silence. That silence was broken only for a couple of seconds by a man's voice—a sad, frail, desperate voice in the distance, barely audible.

"Help. Help," he cried. And that was it. I didn't hear

another word. For the next several seconds, I lay perfectly still, waiting for something else to happen. I don't know what. More pleas for help? More falling debris? Someone to rescue me? But there was nothing. Just complete darkness and utter silence. Which led me to the question I never imagined I would ever have to ask myself, a question I couldn't believe I did not know the answer to.

Was I dead?

I was alone. I could not see anything. I could not hear anything. I was in a lot of pain from head to toe. *If I'm feeling pain,* I thought, *I couldn't be dead, right?* I felt like I was still breathing, but how on earth could I possibly be alive? Didn't a tower just fall on me? I began to wonder if this could all be a really bad dream. I'd had dreams in the past that seemed so real that I actually woke up sweaty and exhausted. If it were a dream, I needed to find a way to bring myself out of it.

I continued to lie there motionless and closed my eyes. I envisioned myself opening them in a few minutes, where I would find myself back under the covers in my bed in Brooklyn with that cool, gentle breeze blowing through my window. Or maybe I'd wake up back home in Trinidad to the sunshine and the sound of the ocean. Anywhere except where I thought I really was. Please. Anywhere.

"Just a dream," I softly and methodically repeated it over and over again, determined to escape the nightmare. "Just a dream. Just a dream . . ."

But it wasn't. And I knew it.

I opened my eyes and stopped trying to fool myself. I was wide awake, buried alive, and absorbed by total darkness. I put my left hand right up to my face, directly in front of my eyes, and couldn't see it. Not even a faint shadow. I touched it to my face, just to reassure myself that my hand was actually there. My right hand and arm were useless, pinned underneath my right side. I had started in that fetal position on my right side when the building was falling, which must have been how my arm ended up under me. I was lying on my right ear with my head jammed between what felt like heavy blocks of concrete. Sharp pains were bouncing around like pinballs through both of my legs. The right one was under the left, which was crushed under what felt like some kind of steel beam. I grunted hard as I tried to squirm around but was getting nowhere. Finally, out of frustration, I screamed as loudly as I could.

"HELLLLLLLLLP!" My voice didn't last long and didn't carry at all. A dry, heaving cough took over, probably because my lungs and mouth were filled with dust. I moved my mouth around to try and create some saliva, then swallowed hard and tried again. Could any of my coworkers hear me? Would they shout back?

"HELP! SOMEBODY HELP!"

It was futile. I was so locked in, probably several feet deep below the surface, that my voice didn't even echo. It was like lying in a sealed coffin. I might as well have been screaming inside my head.

"Nobody can hear you," I said to myself. Yet I continued to shout.

"GET ME OUT! SOMEBODY GET ME OUT OF HERE!" To my surprise, I wasn't crying. I was irritated and getting more frustrated as each second ticked by that nobody responded to me.

"IS THERE ANYBODY OUT THERE? I'M DOWN HERE! SOMEBODY HELP ME! PLEASE HELP ME!" I finally realized how ridiculous I was being. I was running out of breath.

"Okay, Genelle, slow down. Relax," I said, whether out loud or silently I don't know. "Relax and think. Relax and think." After a few minutes of reciting this mantra, I came to only one conclusion: if I was going to have any chance of surviving, I would have to find a way to free myself. I would have to do this on my own. I remained immobile for a while longer to muster up some energy.

"All right," I said to myself with a meager shred of confidence after a few more minutes had passed. "Let's do this."

I tried to wipe some of the dust and grime off my dirty face and out of my sore eyes, hoping that might help me see a glimmer of light. It didn't. I was resigned to the fact that the darkness was there to stay. I then turned my attention to my head. If I could get it free, it would enable to me to move my upper body, and maybe even help me to turn so that I could pull my right arm out from underneath me. I tried to push the huge slab of concrete away from my forehead. It was gritty, and tiny pieces of it came off in my hand, but it would not budge. I then tried to move the piece at the back of my head, but there was no way, because I did not have nearly enough strength to reach backward and push it. There was also a large piece at the top of my head— or maybe it was connected to one of those two pieces in front of and behind me. I couldn't tell, but it also wasn't moving. With that idea shot, I then tried to use my neck muscles to wiggle my head out. All that did was exacerbate my throbbing headache and hurt my scalp since the concrete was holding down clumps of my hair.

I rested for a moment, then focused on my lower body. I wouldn't have known that my right leg, crushed beneath my left leg, was even there had it not been for the pain. I reached down with my left hand and could feel the immense steel beam across me. It wasn't all that was on top of my legs, but it was the one thing I could identify with my sense of touch and what I believed was the heaviest object holding me down. I tried to push it, but to no avail. I attempted to pull it. Yeah, right. I then tried to yank my left leg toward me as I pushed hard on the beam again. I could feel my lower-body muscles straining, but I don't think the leg moved a millimeter. I continued to feel the objects around the beam to see what I could identify. There had to be something I could move. Even if it was something that didn't make a whole lot of difference toward my getting out, it would at least give me some hope and sense of progress.

Then I felt something strange near the back of my left leg, maybe even partly underneath it. It was something soft wrapped in some sort of cloth. I tugged at the material, but it was attached to whatever it was wrapped around. I pulled on it a couple more times, each yank a little harder than the previous. But like everything else so far, it wasn't moving, so I finally just let it go.

The pain in my legs was excruciating. It was like they were being jabbed with hot irons at every point from my thighs to my feet. My head felt like it was swelling as the concrete's grip got stronger and stronger. I tried shifting my body any way that I could, even if just an inch one way or the other, to temporarily ease the pain. It wasn't working.

The only part of me I hadn't tried to free yet was my right arm. I got excited for a moment at the prospect of being able to shake it loose, because then I would have two hands to try and move the concrete and steel that was holding the rest of me down. But what was I thinking? It wasn't going to magically happen. My head was immobile. My legs were smashed flat. I couldn't shift any part of my body at all. With my body pinning the arm down, and my body securely locked in place, how was I going to get that arm out? I wasn't. No way at all.

I rested for a while and thought hard about what to do next. As I quietly meditated, I realized I had two things going for me: a tiny bit of space above me—maybe half-an-arm's length—and the fact that I wasn't claustrophobic. The space gave me a little room to try whatever it was I wanted to do next. And not being claustrophobic—well, that probably kept me from hyperventilating and going insane.

The short rest helped me breathe better, though I could have done without the smell, which was a mixture of smoke and wet rocks. By wet rocks, I mean the sort of odor you'd find by a creek.

After coming to the realization that I'd probably tried everything I could to free myself, and without any success, I decided to shut my eyes again, hoping a short nap would reenergize me and help me push some of the debris off. Why not? It couldn't hurt. I wasn't going anywhere, and nothing else was working. I can honestly say that I still believed I was going to get myself free. I didn't know how, but I still believed I'd escape.

Out of habit, before closing my eyes, I tried to look at my watch to see what time it was. It was still on my left wrist—

loose, but still there. I put it right up to my face, as I had done earlier with my hand. I thought maybe it would be like going to bed at night. At first, when you turn out the lights, it's very dark in the room. After a while, your eyes adjust and it doesn't seem so dark anymore. But my bedroom has lights from the clock, lights from outside, and brightly colored walls. Here I was sealed in a tomb. I could see nothing and never would as long as I was in it.

I put my arm down at my side, shut my eyes, and tried hard to clear my head as I listened to myself breathe. I don't think I actually slept at all. It was more like one of those frustrating half sleeps in which your mind drifts but you're always aware of what is going on around you. I tried to visualize myself escaping, people joyously running to me with open arms, and all the happiness that would come with that. I pictured calling Kimberly and telling her I was alive and envisioned reuniting with Roger. Anything to keep myself in a positive frame of mind. I would guess my "sleep" lasted maybe twenty minutes, when I finally opened my stinging, dust-filled eyes. Nothing had changed. I tried to move each part of me again—head, legs, feet, arm, hand—but couldn't. I was still stuck, still exhausted, still helpless. What else could I do? I didn't own a cell phone. Even if I did, I had no idea where my purse was.

"C'mon, Genelle, think!" I frantically told myself. But if there was anything else I could have done, it was lost on me. I lay there stunned and out of ideas for several minutes, thinking about nothing but the fact that nobody could hear me or see me. I had tried hard to get out on my own but could not do it. The only thing that hurt more than the pain ricocheting through my body was the eerie silence. How could it be so quiet? Where was everybody? How far down was I buried? As I asked those questions, I think shock had taken over my mind. I probably should have been crying, but I wasn't. I just stared at the darkness, fading into despair. Nobody was coming to get me, and there was nothing more I could do.

CHAPTER SEVEN

My Baby

Imagine having a built-in warning signal inside your head—say, a beeping sound—that goes on when you have only a day or so to live. What would your reaction be when you suddenly hear it? Would you panic? Cry? Smile? I think, for most people, it would depend on their age and the kind of life they've led. A one-hundred-year-old lonely woman living in chronic pain who has experienced a full life might welcome it like beautiful, heavenly music and say, "It's about time!" Someone younger, one who has led a good life and has faith that there is something far better waiting in the next life, might make peace with it. But a thirty-year-old woman, full of regrets, would be scared out of her mind, begging for the beeping to stop, frightened of what she'll find on the other side of death. Depression would immediately set in. She'd be overwhelmed by sorrow and guilt, wishing for a do-over.

I could loudly and clearly hear the warning signal in my brain. In the stillness around me, it was *all* I could hear, and I was terrified. I knew death was inevitable—possibly in days, probably in hours, maybe even in minutes. The time was uncertain, but there was no doubt I was in for a slow, painful, isolated demise. There was nothing I could do but quietly lie there and think about everything I was going to miss, everything I did not accomplish, everything I could have done better. And at the forefront of that reflection was Kimberly.

I mentioned that I had left Kimberly in Trinidad to pursue my dream of singing and dancing in New York. It was a dream I'd had since I was a little girl. When I was growing up, my parents, especially my father, were extremely strict. They provided me with what I needed to live, but I could never pursue any of my dreams and was seldom permitted to have any fun. I was a naturally talented dancer and singer but was rarely allowed to show off my skills. The only time my dad would allow me to enter a competition was if there was a chance for me to win money for the family or if it was a school-related event. Otherwise, it was out of the question.

Elvis, too, was strict, very conservative, and did not want me going to clubs or parties with my friends. He was perfectly content coming home from work and doing nothing but hanging out with Kimberly and me. But I was too young and naive to see the value in that. That was a dull life, in my opinion, but the life he expected me to live. The problem was that after years of forcibly living in that type of environment under my parents' stringent rules, I just couldn't do it anymore. After Elvis and I split, even though I had primary custody of Kimberly, I had more freedom to do what I wanted. But it still wasn't enough for me. A large void remained in my life, and I truly believed it was my unfulfilled lifelong dream of turning those triumphant childhood talent competitions into something much bigger. I wanted to perform in the limelight and make it big like all those famous Americans I used to watch on television growing up, and I knew that wasn't going to happen in Trinidad. I finally decided that I needed to do what was best for me and what I told myself would also be best for Kimberly in the long run. In February of 2000, I left Trinidad for the bright lights of New York City. I said good-bye to my eleven-year-old daughter, leaving her behind to live with her father.

Leaving Kimberly with Elvis was, in my mind, temporary. My visa to stay in the United States was good for a year, and I had every intention of sending for her as soon as I possibly could. Maybe I would quickly fall in love with a guy and marry him, and I could send for her then. Somehow, we were going to be reunited soon, but she was going to have to stay back with her dad until I could make that happen.

As one would expect, Kimberly was deeply heartbroken and confused when I left. She was barely eleven and didn't understand how her mother could leave her. I tried to explain my long-term plans for us, but eleven-year-olds live in the present, not the future (a testament to the innocence they still carry). All that mattered to her was that I was no longer there at that moment. I was a couple of thousand miles away, and it hurt her badly. I tried to ease her pain by calling her at least every other night, and on weekends. At first, she refused to talk to me because she was so upset. Her father couldn't even get her to take the phone. But as time went on and she adjusted to life with her dad, a man she dearly loved and whom I trusted to raise her, she started to warm up to me. I visited her twice in Trinidad, and she even came to visit me a couple of times in New York over the summers, most recently in July and August before the towers fell when she was twelve years old. Our times together were wonderful but far too brief for a mother and her daughter. I was determined, though, to stay in New York and make a better life for us . . . well, for me . . . and then I would bring her into it. I looked at the fact that I wasn't with her now as a sacrifice we both had to make, too selfish about my own dreams to realize a child that age should not ever have to sacrifice being raised by her mother, especially for a shot in the dark.

As is often the case for someone attracted to America by the glitz and glamour, I didn't even come close to dancing or singing professionally. Instead, I wound up working hard every day at various blue- and white-collar jobs just to stay afloat—as a nanny, as a secretary, even running wires for a cable company. And instead of aggressively pursuing my dream at night, I pursued the club life of drinking, hanging out with friends, and carousing with guys. I got so hooked on it all that my calls to Kimberly became less and less frequent—from every couple of nights, to just weekends, to weeks in between. I always made up for it, at least in my head, by sending her "stuff" that she couldn't get so easily back home—Barbie dolls, name-brand clothes, top-of-the-line shoes. That was my lame, alternative way of showing her how much I loved her, but it wasn't the kind of love she wanted or needed. I promised her many times that I would come home soon, even though I knew how unlikely that was. I wanted to be with her. I wanted her with me. I wanted to be the good mom I had been back in Trinidad. I really did. But not at the expense of giving up my partying or going back to that quiet, boring life I felt I was forced to live back home.

I was practically blind before the tower fell, but now, wrapped in complete solitude, I could see my life more clearly than ever. I'd failed Kimberly and would likely never have a chance to make any of it up to her. I'd sacrificed our present for an uncertain future, and now we weren't going to get either one with each other. What was she going to go through in the next day or two after finding out about my death? A twelve-year-old child was about to lose her mother forever. It was unbearable to think about her suffering.

I learned later that it didn't take long for the news of the towers' collapse to reach Trinidad. Kimberly was in school when it happened, and her class stopped what they were doing to watch reports about it on television. Just like my cousin in Queens, Kimberly knew I worked in Manhattan but didn't have a clue that I was in the World Trade Center complex. She knew what a huge city it was, which is why it never even crossed her mind that I might have been directly affected by the tragedy.

After school was finished that day, Elvis picked up Kimberly and some of her friends. Kimberly said he had gotten into the daily routine of leaving work, picking them up to take them to the bus station so they could ride home, then going back to work. Elvis was generally a happy person, but according to Kimberly, he was talking in an unusually quiet and solemn voice as he drove the girls to the station that day. He had talked to some people in my family about the attacks, knew that they didn't know my whereabouts, and was aware that there was a chance I could have been in the building during the collapse.

"Are you okay, Dad?" Kimberly asked.

That simple question was all it took for the floodgates to open. He started crying, something Kimberly had never seen him do before. With her friends in the backseat, he quickly regained his composure. Though it was quite obvious to Kimberly that something was bothering him, he didn't want to tell her anything yet since they were about to part ways for several hours until he got home from work that evening.

"I'll be fine," he told her, forcing a little smile as they pulled up to the bus terminal. "You go on home. We'll talk about it later."

Kimberly accepted that. She gave her dad a kiss, then got on the bus with her friends, unaware that her mother was in one of the towers that she and her classmates saw disintegrate on television just a few hours earlier.

As I lay helpless, yearning for my daughter, it hit me hard that I was never going to see her again. I'd sacrificed the last two years with her to chase a dream that I never really tried to reach once I got to New York, and it had cost us our future together. Suddenly, that quiet, boring life back in Trinidad seemed endlessly attractive. But it was too late. I couldn't turn back the clock. All I could do was continue wiping dirt off my face and spitting it out of my mouth; to endure the terrible pain in my head and legs, thinking about how badly I'd screwed up.

CHAPTER EIGHT

Clarity

As I had done with Kimberly, I allowed my selfishness to inch its way into my relationship with Roger. I was addicted to the nightlife of New York and just couldn't bring myself to give it up, even for a man I loved. Sometimes Roger went to the clubs with me. He enjoyed a good party, too, but he had a problem with my excess.

"Why do you have to go every single Friday night?" he would often ask when the end of the week rolled around and I'd be making plans with my friends to hit the town. And, of course, the partying continued on Saturday and often into the early hours of Sunday.

"Because it's what I like to do," I would carelessly respond. "It's how I relax after a long week of work." And so I continued going out, enjoying the drinking and dancing, and he continued to reluctantly tolerate it. I knew that I meant everything to him, just like he did to me. He was always there for me unconditionally—and he was there for me again on September 11, waiting for me to come out of the building.

Roger told me later that after we had made arrangements that morning to meet outside at Century 21, he walked over from his office. It took him about twenty minutes, just as he expected. It was probably about 9:30 a.m. When he first arrived, his attention was captured by all the sirens blaring from the dozens of fire trucks, police cars, and ambulances. They were everywhere, as the Twin Towers in front of him continued to steadily burn near the top. At first he could mentally handle what he saw because he was seeing what he expected to see. But as the minutes ticked by, everything around him got progressively worse.

He quickly realized it was no small plane, or planes, that had slammed into the buildings. There was a jet engine lying on the ground, just a few yards from the storefront, along with several huge pieces of twisted, broken metal that appeared to be from a large aircraft. That area had been cordoned off by police, who were whisking people past it. Most didn't have to be convinced to move along, because they were trying to flee. So many of them, in suits and dresses torn by debris, were gashed and cut, some more severely than others. But, according to Roger, very few people seemed to be asking for help. They just wanted to get as far away from the site as possible. It was turning into an ugly, ugly scene, but it was nothing compared to what Roger and his fellow onlookers witnessed next . . . something that no human being could ever be prepared for.

Roger heard screams ring out from nearby. Then he heard a thud. And more screams. And another thud. And . . .

He looked up to the black, burning sky and saw people falling out of windows, one after the other. There had to be dozens of them dropping from the floors near where the smoke and flames were shooting out, maybe ninety or a hundred stories above the ground. But considering how many people there were and the fact that the top floors of the building were still standing, he came to the ghastly realization that they weren't falling out—they were willfully jumping to their deaths, landing on the ground just yards away from him.

They kept falling, one after another, as he described it, almost as if they were taking turns. He knew there was no way any of those people could have thought they would survive if they jumped from that elevation. They had to know they were leaping to their deaths, which made Roger realize just how horrifying it must have been up there.

Enormously distressed, he tried to call me at my desk a couple of times, but his cell had no reception. He yelled my name and searched for me on the streets. Injured people continued to race past him. Bodies continued to fall from above. He knew I should have been out long ago. It was now a few minutes before 10 a.m., and the calm demeanor he'd displayed earlier that morning had turned to pure panic.

"GENELLE! GENELLE!" He shouted my name repeatedly. He stayed close to our meeting place, frantically pacing a few yards in each direction, trying to spot me. He gravitated back to the front of Century 21 and pulled his phone out again, hoping for those few bars that would give him the signal to contact me.

With nothing there, he slipped the phone back into his pocket.

That's when the ground under him started to rumble.

He looked at some people standing next to him, who were pointing up. Roger followed their fingers to the sky and couldn't believe his eyes. The South Tower was falling.

"RUUUUUUUN!" He heard someone howl. Screams echoed from every direction. Roger turned from the tower and ran as fast as he could. He looked behind him and saw nothing but an exploding cloud of dust chasing him. He continued running until he felt the pressure of the cloud at his back, like an angry dog about to bite. He sharply turned and barged through the door of a convenience store down the block.

"Lock the door!" the owner shouted to him, wanting to make sure the rolling debris didn't force the door open. There were probably a couple dozen people already in the store seeking refuge. Just as Roger turned the lock, another man who had been running behind him pounded hysterically on the glass.

"Let me in! Please let me in!!"

Roger unlocked the door, let him in, then quickly shut and locked it again as the wave of white dust went flying by the storefront. The man was covered in the dust from head to toe, Roger later described, and looked as white as a ghost. Roger and some of the others brushed him off as best they could before they brusquely migrated toward the back to get as far from the destruction as possible. Roger tried his phone again. Still not working. He talked to some of the others in the store, a few of them crying as they tried to figure out what was going on.

"I was supposed to meet my girlfriend outside the building," Roger said desperately to the group. "She was in the North Tower."

Some of the people there with him had been inside the towers, but none of them knew me. They all shared their stories of where they were, what they saw, whom they were supposed to meet. Those who had cell phones had no reception. The owner told them to help themselves to some bottled water. They could do nothing but wait for the dust to settle so they could go back out and start searching for their loved ones again. But their nightmare was only just beginning. They had been in there for about thirty minutes when the ground began rumbling again.

It was the North Tower . . . my tower . . . crumbling to pieces. Roger couldn't see it from where he was, but he knew what was happening as a fresh cloud of dust, just like the first one, stormed past the store.

He waited until the dust thinned out a bit and then, unable to idly stay in the store any longer, grabbed a rag that was lying nearby, covered his nose and mouth, and rushed out the door. Swept up in the remaining dust, he ran with its flow, away from the towers, pulling his phone out of his pocket and keeping his squinting eyes on it until he had reception. Once he did, he stopped in his tracks and called his brother Corey who worked about a block away and was watching everything unfold from the rooftop of his building.

Roger gave Corey a brief synopsis of what had transpired that morning—from the initial phone call I made to Roger, to his waiting for me outside my building.

"Do you know if she got out?" Corey asked.

"She should have," Roger said, "but I don't know."

"Okay. Meet me over here at my office and we'll go find her."

"All right," Roger replied. "I'm going to run back to my office first and see if she called me there. My cell phone hasn't been working until now."

That typically twenty-minute walk took about ten minutes as Roger sprinted to his office. When he got there, he went straight for his office phone and checked it. No messages.

"Where are you, Genelle?" he desperately whispered, starting to think the worst. He sat down in his chair, dejected, staring at the phone, trying to will it to ring. Of course, it never did.

Roger, covered in dust and grime, left his office after a few minutes and hustled a few blocks over to Corey's building to meet his brother.

"Have you heard anything?" Corey said.

"Nothing," Roger said.

"We're going to find her," Corey promised.

The thought that I could have still been in the building when it came down was jabbing at Roger's brain, but he told me later that he simply refused to believe it. After all, he reasoned, the building did not collapse until over an hour after we agreed to meet at Century 21. Even if I had casually walked all the way down the steps, I would have gotten out in plenty of time.

"Some people here have suggested that we check out St. Vincent's Hospital and see if she's been admitted there," Corey said. "Let's walk over there and see what we find."

Roger had never thought of that. St. Vincent's Hospital was in Greenwich Village and would probably be one of the primary hospitals where victims were taken.

When they arrived there, they were met with complete chaos. People were milling around everywhere, some, like Roger, looking for loved ones, others covered in blood, waiting patiently to be treated. Roger found a woman at a reception desk who was keeping a list of people brought in from the towers.

"I'm looking for Genelle Guzman," Roger said to her.

She scanned the list, then shook her head.

"I'm sorry, there's nobody here with that name."

"How about Judy Guzman," he said hopefully, trying to cover all his bases.

"Sorry," she replied.

After overhearing stories and rumors from people in the waiting room, Roger really didn't know what to conclude about me. Some people had made it out. Some were dead. Some were trapped under the rubble. Some were simply nowhere to be found.

"Let's go home," Roger said to Corey dejectedly. He couldn't think of anything else to do. With the transportation system in the city pretty much shut down in every respect, Roger and Corey headed by foot for the Brooklyn Bridge. Once they crossed into Brooklyn, they were fortunate enough to hail a cab, which took them to our apartment. The brothers didn't say a whole lot to each other during the ride. Roger just did a lot of thinking.

He feared that I was dead. But there was that one caveat that kept nagging at him: I had more than an hour to get out. How could I not be out? He ran different scenarios through his mind. Maybe I saw the people all bloodied like he did and just took off. Maybe I left with somebody who needed help. Maybe I was at another hospital. There were a lot of "maybes" but nothing else to hang his hopes on.

While Roger would have been heartbroken by my disappearance no matter what the state of our relationship at the time, there was an extra sting to his sorrow because, as I mentioned before, we had recently reconciled from the fight we'd been in about two weeks earlier. The fight stemmed from my feeling that Roger was too controlling, always telling me what to do, never giving me the space to be the person I wanted to be. I called him selfish. It was no different, in my mind, than being back in Trinidad with Elvis or my parents. The argument got so intense that I told him it was over, and I left him and went to live with my niece, Carla, in Queens. I was serious about not going back to him. I wasn't going to be suffocated like that anymore, I'd proclaimed. After just a day or two of my absence, Roger called me at Carla's place every day for two weeks, asking me to come back. I was stubborn at first and refused to talk to him, but I finally gave in. After some very long discussions on the phone, followed by even longer discussions face-to-face, we patched things up over the weekend with the agreement that he'd give me some room to breathe.

How ironic.

Here I was now, all alone under the rubble, nobody anywhere near me, with literally almost no room to breathe. I knew then that I had been the selfish one. I finally understood what it was that Roger wanted—simply to live a happy and peaceful life with the woman he loved and not have to compete with the dancing and drinking and flirtations from other men. It was the simple, little things that mattered to him. It is the simple and little things that usually make relationships last. Why was that so difficult for me to understand before this hopeless moment? And who was I kidding? I loved him too, so much. But I had taken him for granted.

CHAPTER NINE

Evil

I guess it was noon or one, maybe even two in the afternoon—I obviously had no idea for sure—when everything around me started getting very hot. Not hot to the touch, but the air temperature was rapidly rising. Warm beads of sweat were forming on my scraped-up forehead. My left arm and hand, caked in dirt, were getting sticky. My throat was bone dry and sore. That wet-rock smell—what was its source? Was there water somewhere near me? What I would give for just a splash of it on my desiccated tongue. Anything to relieve my dry, parched throat.

I felt like I was in an oven. The warmth was intensifying every few seconds, and the oven door was locked. I tried futilely to push on the hard, heavy debris that was above me, thinking I might find a way to create some sort of ventilation. Of course, nothing moved. I smacked it a few times with my palm. Still nothing. I then lightly punched it while visualizing my fist cracking it open, creating a hole large enough for all the hot air to rise through. At least my imagination was still working.

I shifted my train of thought and began to wonder if all the heat I was feeling was partly self-inflicted. I'm sure I was dehydrated, since a sip of hot chocolate at my desk and a tiny cup of water when I brushed my teeth in the morning were all the liquids I'd ingested since Monday. There was no breeze. No air circulation whatsoever. Throw in all the exhaustive work I was doing as I tried to shift my body around and bust a hole through the top, and all the worrying I was doing that was undoubtedly raising my blood pressure—that's a lot of heat with nowhere for it to escape. I decided to lie perfectly still for a while to see if that would cool me down. I kept my eyes open to help me stay awake and concentrated on listening to my breathing, which wasn't difficult considering it was the only sound I could hear. I inhaled gently, but deeply, through my nose, barely tolerating the stench that came with it. I exhaled slowly through my mouth, occasionally protruding my lower lip so that my breath climbed up my face to my forehead, where the combination of sweat and air offered a brief reprieve from the heat.

"Think pleasant thoughts," I said to myself. "Pleasant thoughts. You're going to get out of here. Just relax. Just relax."

But that was impossible to do for more than a few seconds. The thought of Kimberly made me smile. The thought of her growing up without her mom made me cringe. The thought of Roger and the positive turn our relationship had taken was wonderful, but knowing he was probably standing just a block or two away from me and unable to see or hear me was agonizing. There was Rosa's comment when we were going down the stairwell, the one about my shoes, that made me laugh. Where was Rosa? Buried alive like me, or dead? I thought about the others in our group in that stairwell—Susan, Pasquale, the Russian man . . . my heart was breaking with each name. I thought about my family, many of them back in Trinidad, one of the most beautiful places on the planet. But even thinking about home didn't offer me solace for very long. While I had so many good memories of growing up there, there were also some very confusing times, especially related to my faith.

Besides being baptized in the Catholic faith, I also received the sacraments of First Reconciliation, Holy Communion, and Confirmation. I went to a Catholic school my whole life. We prayed as a family before dinner each night. Crucifixes hung from our walls. Mom kept a rosary next to her bed and used it quite often. We never missed Sunday Mass. Our priest was a good friend of the family. It was a faith with a lot of tradition and ceremony that surrounded every aspect of my daily life . . . but a faith I never consistently embraced.

Why not?

There were several reasons, the biggest being a sin that was right in front of my eyes every day. My parents were together for forty years, and they had ten children. So what's wrong with that? I mean, God says in the very first book of the Bible, Genesis, to "be fruitful and multiply." But notice that I said my parents were "together" for forty years. They were never married, and I have absolutely no idea why not. I never asked. I did not know what their reasoning would be, and I was too scared to find out. For some of my childhood, I didn't even know they weren't married. I just assumed they were. I think, at times, they even referred to each other as husband and wife. But when I found out the truth, I really struggled to accept it. How could they preach to me about being a good Catholic girl and avoiding sin when I was taught in school that, in the eyes of God, they were living in sin every day? And yet they went to church each week and received Holy Communion. Wasn't receiving the body of Christ with that kind of sin on their souls another sin? And if they were going to confession on a regular basis like they should have, were they not confessing that sin each time? There were too many contradictions in my parents' behavior that I just didn't understand and couldn't get past to fully respect the faith.

We had Kimberly baptized in Elvis's Pentecostal church and attended services there each week. I went because I knew he wanted me to go, and it was an easy way to keep the peace between us. I was also not far removed from living with my family where I went to church every week anyway, so other than some differences between the Catholic and Pentecostal faiths, it wasn't a major change in my life. But I was no different than my parents. I was living in sin, with a child out of wedlock, and going to church. I felt like such a hypocrite.

And what could I do about it now?

The temperature didn't feel like it was rising anymore, but it also wasn't dropping at all. It was stagnant and barely tolerable, which wasn't getting me anywhere. All it meant was that I might not die of heat exhaustion, or at least not as quickly. Maybe a lack of nutrition would take my life instead? I wasn't even hungry. Thirsty, yes. But what did it matter anyway? Death was death.

"GET ME OUT OF HERE!" I blurted out with an angry, frustrated tone as I once again slapped the rubble above me, knowing it wasn't going to budge but hoping someone might hear the slapping. "Can anybody hear me? Hello? SOMEBODY HELP ME!" I stopped yelling and closed my eyes and held my breath, listening intently for a response to my pleas. Any noise at all. A voice. A rustle. A peep.

Nothing.

That short outburst started to make me warmer again. But there had to be something besides me creating all that heat. I couldn't be making it that hot that quickly. Then it occurred to me: did the collapse of the building create fires? I did smell smoke. In fact, I would think there had to be fires with all the electricity, and probably gas lines, running through the building. There was also a parking garage underground. With all of that gasoline, cars must have exploded, with the heat from them seeping up through the debris. And what about the wet-rock smell? It could have been from all the water in the building's pipes. Or maybe it was water from fire trucks trying to put the fires out. But wouldn't I have heard the trucks, or even the spray of the water? My God, how deeply buried was I? Maybe there weren't any fires at all. Maybe I was close enough to the surface that the afternoon heat from the sun was being absorbed by the debris. But then why couldn't I hear anything or see any light? Many questions, no answers—all frustrating.

Then there was another possibility that I couldn't get out of my mind: that this was the first phase of my entrance into hell. As bizarre as that idea may sound, it's not so crazy when you're buried alive, hurting in every way possible, and unsure about your salvation. I'd been taught as a child that hell was real, an eternal existence of pain, often signified by flames and heat. And now that I thought about it, the hotter I got, the more everything about me seemed to hurt. A stinging sensation continued to flow up and down my legs. My head throbbed like a drum getting pounded at a rock concert. My throat was drier than a desert. Was this really a taste of hell?

I was physically and mentally worn out. I flowed in and out of consciousness, trying to stay awake, trying to overcome the heat, desperately trying to think of anything more I could do to give myself a chance to survive. But all positive thoughts were gone. Hell was all I could think about.

The irony about my life was that I always believed in God. I really did. It was difficult not to, considering His teachings were thrust upon me daily at home, in school, and at church. But with all the conflicting feelings I had about my faith, I was one of those who only acknowledged Him in two situations: if I was forced to, such as through school prayer or religion class, or if I wanted something. If I wanted something as a child, I didn't hesitate to ask Him for it. If I was in a predicament that I knew I couldn't get myself out of, or that wasn't going the way I wanted it to, I never hesitated to ask Him to step in and take care of the situation. I believed He was always there, always invisibly around me, but the sad thing is that I never prayed when I didn't need something. I never built any kind of personal relationship with Him. I went through all the motions but never sought anything deeper. And I only drifted further from Him as I grew up, not even praying when I needed something. Sure, I might have prayed, "Oh, God, help me through this," but I never gave any deep thought to whom

I was praying. It was really just an expression. I treated Him more like a genie in a bottle than as my creator. And I certainly never considered praising Him and thanking Him after I got what I wanted.

What would it take, at this point, to get Him to hear me? There were billions of people in the world, people much better than I, who rightly deserved His attention more than I did. Did He care about me at all? If so, had He given up on me? Would He even bother listening to me if I tried to talk to Him?

If He did care, He never would have put me in this situation, right?

Stop. Here I was, again, selfishly thinking about me. What about all the other people caught in the building when it collapsed? There had to be good people trapped in there who died. No way could most people survive under the collapse of a building. Assuming that was the case, why did He let this happen to them and keep me alive to this point? He had to have a reason. If I only knew how to talk to Him about this, how to talk to Him without being self-centered. I was so confused, so desperate, so . . . just so sad. Sad that I was born and raised to believe in Him, yet I didn't even know how to pray. Sad that I was ignorant for so long and didn't realize it until it was too late.

My life was nearing its end, probably at least fifty years sooner than I would have ever imagined, and I felt no connection to God. For the first time since I'd been buried in this hell hole, I cried. Through all the physical pain, as tired as I was, as thirsty as I was, I had not cried once. But now, finally realizing how I'd so often wasted my days, I broke down. Growing up, I had been slowly walking a road toward hell with my ignorance about God and had picked up the pace as I ignored Him in adulthood. Now I was at the very end of that road, standing on hell's doorstep. It seemed only natural now to take those last couple of steps through that door and live the eternally damned life that I deserved. It was the simplest choice at this point. I could feel the devil welcoming me.

But was it my only choice?

With that question now resting on the tip of my brain, I wiped away the few tears my dehydrated body was able to produce and thought about it. Was it possible to turn around and see if I could make my way back up this road toward God? How could it be? It felt much too late. Or was it? My mind was scrambled as my thoughts strayed in every direction. This all would have been so much simpler if I had just followed God from the beginning like I was taught . . . but I hadn't.

I was getting too worked up, too intense. I needed to stop asking myself so many questions, stop asking, "What if . . . ?" It was getting me nowhere. I just needed to calm down, collect my thoughts, and do something to change the sinful course I'd been on for so long. But what could I do?

CHAPTER TEN

Miracles

Still clueless as to where I was, Roger and Corey arrived at our apartment to a small gathering of people already there waiting for them—their sister, Camille, who was visiting from Trinidad, along with some friends who had heard about Roger's plight as word quickly spread by phone. Roger was dismayed, but not surprised, to find that I was not one of those waiting for him. They all gave him a hug and assured him that I was okay. He forced a smile, knowing that probably wasn't true.

They solemnly entered the apartment and turned on the television, watching the endless news reports. The home phone and some of the others' cell phones continually rang, and Roger prayed each time that I would be on the other end. But with each call, Roger only became more depressed. He knew every second that ticked by without his seeing or hearing from me increased the chances that I did not survive. He got up from his chair and stood before his friends and family.

"Guys," he despondently said to everyone, "I appreciate your coming over, but I need to be alone now."

He did not, however, ask them to leave. Instead, it was he who left. He wandered into the kitchen, opened the cupboard where we kept some liquor, and removed a full bottle of rum. He looked at it for a moment, thought about getting a glass, but saw no reason to. The others just watched, not sure what to say, and too afraid to stop him. He went into our bedroom, gently closed the door behind him, and sat on the bed. With tears streaming down his cheeks, he unscrewed the cap of the bottle. As he took it off, he looked up and gently called upon God for help. He begged God to save me. Roger believed in God and prayed occasionally. Like me, he was born and raised Catholic, but he was not a regular churchgoer.

He looked down at the bottle of rum in his hand, raised it to his lips, tilted his head back, and took a giant swig. He then leaned back against the headboard and continued to cry. It would be the next day before he would come out of the bedroom.

Probably about the same time that Roger was mourning, my head was badly aching from all the heat, crying, and thoughts of hell. I was exhausted, but I didn't want to go to sleep. I knew that my time was running out, and sleeping was the last thing I could afford to do. I was also terrified that if I did doze off, I might never wake up—at least on earth. I tried to compromise with myself by closing my eyes while strongly concentrating on other possible ways to get out. I figured if I kept the brain waves flowing with ideas, I'd stay semiconscious. But it didn't work. I fell asleep, and for a long time.

When I finally woke up, I was very restless. My eyes were sore, and my mind was back to cranking out terrifying thoughts of what miserable fate awaited me. It didn't feel like I'd been out for very long because it had not been a relaxing nap, but I knew it had been longer than it felt because as quickly as the temperature had risen before I fell asleep, it was now falling. The cooling air felt refreshing at first, but within only minutes it had dropped past that comfort zone and gotten ice cold. It was so bitterly freezing that my teeth were chattering. My once-warm, sweat-covered skin was now irritatingly clammy. I reached more than once with my left hand toward the lower end of my body, as if I'd find a blanket, like on my comfy bed at home. But all I found was that same piece of raw steel. I felt all around for anything loose that I could put on top of me to keep warm. I stretched my arm behind my left leg, the same spot where I'd felt that soft cloth earlier. I tugged a little harder at it than I did the last time but still couldn't pull it free.

Why was it suddenly so cold? Were the fires put out? Maybe it was night. The sun usually started to set about 7 p.m.

Had it really been more than eight hours? My watch was still uselessly dangling on my wrist. I touched the small, round, cold glass of it to my nose, as if I'd be able to feel the hands of the clock. I then held it right up to my eyes and stared at it intently, but the darkness wouldn't let up at all.

As each minute continued to tick away, I got more and more frightened like at no other time in my life. It was as if Satan was messing with me in every way possible. This whole quandary started that morning with the optimistic notion that I was going to get out of the building safely, but my effort to escape was thwarted by the tower's collapse while I was on the thirteenth-floor landing. How about that? Of all the floors I could have been on when it fell, I was on unlucky number thirteen. Unbelievable. Then I'm buried alive with no way out, but still conscious and in a fully functional mental state so that I could feel and understand every ounce of physical and mental pain, which included going from extreme heat to extreme cold. I was left to think about all the mistakes I had made in my life with no opportunity to fix them. This was torture. I imagined Satan just loving every minute of it, playing me like some sick video game, sending more and more evil my way, racking up the points in his evil little world every time I suffered a little more. And I wasn't the only victim in evil's sinister plot. Similar evil had befallen everybody else in the building. How many lives had been destroyed? How many others were being tortured like me? Only by some implausible miracle would I escape this torment.

Miracle! That's it! That word triggered something—something good—in my meandering mind. I think I stunned myself so much with the thought of that word that I actually moved my head a little bit from the jaws of the concrete. Miracle. The word was a golden key that unlocked a piece of my past and could affect my future. How did that story go? It was when I was a little girl back in Trinidad and my aunt Hilda was diagnosed with something. What was it?

Think, Genelle, think!

I couldn't remember, but it was bad. Not cancer, but another disease or condition that seemed to be eating away at her life. She was hurting, constantly wailing. I'm sure she was on some kind of medication, but it was no match for the pain she was feeling. It was awful. I recall my mother taking me to my aunt's house to visit her almost every day. I loved my aunt but hated seeing her in that state. Mom would do everything she could to make her comfortable during the time we were there and would always take a few minutes to pray over her before we left. I stood back and watched with curiosity each time Mom prayed. On some of those days, people would come over from our church and pray with Mom, putting their hands on my aunt's head as they did. It was kind of weird and surreal. They did this for days, and I didn't understand the point. Aunt Hilda obviously wasn't getting any better. In fact, by the agony she constantly exhibited, I would say she was getting worse each day. I thought it was a miracle that she was even still alive, but I don't think anybody else saw it that way. Why would God keep someone alive when she was in so much pain? Why not just bring her up to heaven? I was convinced that He wasn't listening to the prayers to make her better and that her time to go was coming. Or . . . was He, in fact, listening?

One day, with several people from the church surrounding her, a priest came into the house. He was a very nice man with a presence about him that made everybody feel like anything was possible. He sat down next to my aunt and talked with her for a while in a very soothing voice, helping her to calm down a little bit and making everybody in the room feel more comfortable. He then put his hand on top of her head and said a prayer. A few prayers, actually. I don't know what they were. He was talking quickly and quietly, almost in a mumble. I wish now that I knew what he said, because, within seconds after he was finished, Aunt Hilda completely stopped crying. There was a hush across the room. Was she dead? No, I could see her eyes were open. The priest slid his chair away from her bed as everybody watched in stunned silence. Aunt Hilda got a confused look on her face and stared at the priest as if to say, "What did you just do?" With everyone, including me, as a witness, she slowly sat up. The silence was broken with gasps from everybody in the room. Aunt Hilda cracked a smile, the first one we'd seen in forever. Just like that, the pain was gone! Just like that! For the first time in a long time, my aunt appeared to have her life back. I couldn't believe what I was seeing. Cries of "It's a miracle!" shot around the room as everybody hugged and kissed the priest, my aunt, and one another. It was an incredible, amazing experience that made an indelible mark in my mind.

I don't know what happened that day. Did our priest have some kind of special power? Did God really work a miracle through him? There's always the chance it was coincidental, that the medication finally kicked in when the priest came over. Maybe Aunt Hilda wasn't as sick as she thought. Maybe a lot of the pain was in her mind, and simply seeing the priest and thinking that he was healing her with his prayers was all she needed to restore her faith in her health. I don't know. What I'm certain of, though, is that something totally unexpected and incredibly good happened to her, and it happened after a lot of prayer by some very faith-filled people who never gave up hope. I believed then that I had witnessed a miracle. And that's why I was so excited to think of the word "miracle" and that wonderful memory. If a miracle could happen once, it could happen again, right?

But the difference between then and now, I reminded myself, was that I didn't have people praying over me, caring for me, and surrounding me with their love like Aunt Hilda did. There was no priest at my side to intervene between God and me. Maybe there were people out on the streets of New York, or in their homes across the country and in Trinidad, praying for me and everybody else who was in the building, but was it enough to create a miracle?

I decided I might be my sole supplicator. It was my responsibility to reach out directly, and with no mediators, to the God I had neglected for so long. I needed to throw myself at His mercy and own up to my mistakes, something I'd never done before. The drinking. The partying. Leaving my daughter behind. Were all those things sins? I wasn't sure that each was a horrible act on its own. People drink. People party. I left my daughter with the intent of making a better life for us here and reuniting with her soon—even if the term "better life" was much more subjective than I realized. Still, altogether, my decisions had reflected an extremely self-absorbed person who put her own pleasures ahead of everyone, including God, and was not living a life God would find acceptable. I could probably pick out a few of the Ten Commandments I hadn't kept, either. In that moment, I could think of one commandment I'd broken in particular.

I certainly wouldn't have called myself a liar, but there was one lie I'd been telling and living over and over for several months and, again, for purely selfish reasons. I mentioned earlier that I came to America in February of 2000 and that my visa was good for a year. Well, for about the last seven months, I had been living in the country illegally. The way the visa worked was that I was supposed to return to Trinidad on my own when it expired. If I didn't, then when I did decide to return to my country, the odds were that I would never again be granted another visa. I knew it had expired, and I knew I was supposed to go home, but I did everything I could not to let anybody else know. And it wasn't easy. When I started working through the temp agency, the human resources department there pestered me for months for various pieces of documentation, and my excuses as to why I could not provide that information ran the gamut: I lost it; I got mugged and they stole my documents; my attorney had it. I probably even blamed my dog at some point, even though I didn't have a dog. It was ridiculous what excuses I came up with and got away with, but I was determined to stay in this country and eventually send for Kimberly. I truly thought one year would be long enough to make that happen. It wasn't. I know how wrong and foolish it was of me to not play by the rules, but I was arrogant enough to think that I could get away with it.

I decided that this was it. This was where I had to begin if God was even going to give me the time of day—which was quickly dwindling—and consider a miracle for me. I had to lay it all out on the table. I had to look at this makeshift grave I was buried in as a confessional and I had to believe that God was listening . . . and that He cared. But it had to be more than words. I couldn't just confess my sins, say I was sorry, toss in a Hail Mary or two, and wait for the debris to open up above me. There had to be substance to it. I had to mean it. It had to come from the heart. Could I do that? Could I even figure out how after all these years? Would it mean anything to Him, or would it just come across as a desperate, empty plea? And really, does God even work that way? Can someone faithfully reach out to Him in a time of need and expect Him to come to the rescue? I know there are plenty of people who have been in dire straits who have begged God for help, only to feel as though He didn't answer their pleas. But pleading was my only option. I needed to try.

Somehow, for some reason, through all of this spiritual thinking, the iciness of the air had subsided. It was no longer extremely cold or extremely hot. It was comfortable, as comfortable as being buried underground could be. Why? What happened? What changed? Was God already listening to my thought process? Did He know what I was about to try to do? Whatever the reason, I needed to appreciate it and thankfully accept every break I could get, no matter how small, while keeping my focus on God. I was still thirsty, still tired, still keenly aware that I was standing at the doors of hell, but I felt reenergized after thinking about what happened to my aunt. There was a chance. There was hope. Maybe slim, but it was there. And it was there because I came to the understanding that I was not going to get out on my own, like I arrogantly assumed I would when this all started many hours before. I finally realized that it needed to start with me but would ultimately end with Him.

So where to begin? How does one talk to God, especially someone like me who hadn't talked to Him in so long? I tried to think of the perfect words, but they weren't materializing. I thought that perhaps I could just start with a standard prayer. No. Too formal, too canned. This needed to be personal. It needed to be sincere. I needed to hurry up that road to the heavenly door at the other end, knock on it, and ask if I could come in. How do I do that?

Just start speaking, Genelle, I said to myself in my mind. *Just start speaking to Him.* And so I did.

"God, it's Genelle," I said timidly. "I'm in a difficult situation right now, one that I got myself into, and I need Your help."

My mother always told me to "live the life of the Lord," but it never fazed me how crucial that was until this moment. Never did I imagine that my fate would be out of my hands. But it was. I needed help. The Lord's help. And I felt like I had just taken a huge step in the right direction by admitting it. It was a strangely freeing experience.

CHAPTER ELEVEN

Prayer

When Elvis returned home from work, Kimberly says she was there anxiously waiting for him, very curious to know what had him so upset earlier when he picked her up from school. She could tell by her dad's glum demeanor when he walked in the door that whatever was wrong was still bothering him. But he didn't say anything to her right away. I think he was still trying to figure out exactly how to say it. After about thirty minutes of silence, he finally approached her.

"Kimberly, I need to tell you something that is going to be very difficult to hear," he said hesitantly.

"What's up, Dad?" she asked.

"You saw what happened in New York today—with the buildings?"

"Yeah, we watched it in school," she said. He started to cry like he had that afternoon, surely confusing her even more.

"Well," Elvis said, "You need to know that your mother worked in one of those towers that fell."

Kimberly just stared at him as she tried to process what he told her.

"You mean she got out, right?" she asked with an incredulous look.

Elvis cried some more.

"I don't know," he said. "Nobody has been able to find her."

Kimberly continued to stare in disbelief. She let out an uncomfortable laugh from the shock of the news.

"So if you don't know where she is, then you're saying she's probably dead?"

Elvis put his arms around her and continued to cry. Kimberly was stunned. After a few seconds, her brain processed it all, and she let out a yell . . . then fainted in his arms. He woke her up to make sure she was okay, then carried her to her room and let her sleep through dinner. A couple of hours later, when she woke up, she told him about a strange dream she had.

"You told me Mom was in one of the towers that fell, and I laughed and asked if she was dead, and . . ."

"Kimberly, that wasn't a dream," he said gravely. "They're still searching for your mother." She was stunned all over again as she stared blankly at him.

"No. No," she said, shaking her head. Elvis hugged her and held her for a long time as father and daughter cried together.

While the sadness of my probable death was gripping my family and friends, from New York to Trinidad, I continued trying to make the long, uphill journey back toward the God I'd been introduced to when I was young but had lost almost all contact with. I continued to speak to Him, as if we were just having a conversation. Even though I knew that He knew my story, I told it to Him as if He'd never heard it. I explained everything: why I didn't pray to Him when I was younger unless I needed something; why I was in this country illegally; why I left my daughter; why I partied so much; why I drank so much; why I was living and sleeping with my boyfriend when we weren't married. I wasn't making any excuses. I was simply giving Him the facts and explaining why I had lived the life I had lived.

"Now that I've told You all of this, Lord, I want You to know how sorry I am, and that every bit of it is going to change," I said, gaining more and more confidence as I spoke. "From now on, I won't come to You only when I need something. I will clear up my illegal status as soon as I get out of here and go back to Trinidad if I have to. I will be the mother to my daughter that I should have been these last couple of years. The drinking and partying will stop. And if Roger is the one for me, I will marry him and not just live with him."

It was a lot. I admit that. While it may sound like I was biting off more than I could chew and making outrageous promises that would be nearly impossible to fulfill—not to mention presuming that this prayer would be the key to my escape—I was very sincere about every word. I wasn't trying to fool myself or Him. And I wasn't trying to bargain with Him. I honestly felt the repentance in my heart.

Now that I felt like I was making progress in building a rapport with Him, I decided to say some common prayers that I said each Sunday in church when I went as a child. I guess you could call them a penance, of sorts.

"Our Father, who art in heaven, hallowed be Thy name. Thy kingdom come, Thy will be done . . ."

I probably said the Lord's Prayer about five or six times. The first couple of times I was focused more on getting the words exactly right—it had been a while. Then I focused on what I thought the words meant and how they played into my life. I don't know if I had the meanings right or not, but I was trying.

"Our Father, who art in heaven, hallowed be Thy name." It goes back to that genie-in-a-bottle mentality I used to have. I never really learned, or made an effort to learn, how to pray to Him. As I've said, He was merely someone I called out to when I needed something, and I rarely thanked him for anything He did for me. I hadn't looked at my relationship with Him as a two-way street. That way of thinking had to change, and now.

"Thy kingdom come, Thy will be done, on earth as it is in heaven." What is God's will? I'm pretty sure it's not wasting my life hanging out at the clubs and getting drunk every weekend, completely passed out through Sunday mornings while other people are going to church, and trying to rid myself of a hangover just in time to go back to work each Monday. I could simply no longer put off living the way I knew I should be living. I needed to live a life pleasing to the Lord now so that, if I die tomorrow, which was a distinct possibility, I would be prepared to enter His kingdom.

"Give us this day our daily bread." How often did I take that for granted? Food wasn't plentiful, growing up in a house of twelve, but we always had it. Since dinner Monday night, the only thing I'd eaten was a bite of a bagel. I wasn't starving, probably because I was so thirsty and had other things to worry about, but I did need food. Without it, my cause of death would probably be starvation. How many times did I say this prayer as a kid and just glaze over that line? Always.

"And forgive us our trespasses." When was the last time I'd gone to confession? Probably years ago when I was forced to go in school. And whether I went to confession or not, I could have, at the very least, tried to talk to God myself about my wrongdoings. But that didn't happen until now. Having spilled my transgressions to God, I needed to believe that He would forgive me and that I could start with a clean slate. And I needed to work hard at keeping that slate as pristine as possible.

"As we forgive those who trespass against us." I've never been one to hold grudges, at least not for too long. But now, after saying these words while facing death, I realized even more that life is far too short to stay angry at somebody. I was so grateful that Roger and I mended our differences before this tragedy. How much worse would I feel right now if he and I hadn't been speaking to each other when this happened?

"And lead us not into temptation, but deliver us from evil." This line would be my biggest challenge. What will I do if I get out of here and am invited to celebrate my new life by having drinks at a bar? What will I do if my employer continues to ask for my paperwork on my citizenship, knowing that I risk being deported if I tell the truth? I genuinely felt like I would do the right thing. But did I feel that way because of my desperate situation? If given the chance to live, I would have the chance to prove my sincerity. Until then, all I could do was continue to pray and continue to trudge back up that road toward God, away from evil's grasp.

How had I ignored that prayer all of my life? What a simple, straightforward prayer. I couldn't see how I could go wrong if I kept it at the forefront of my mind in everything I did.

I continued with some other prayers I knew, or sort of knew, ones I had learned as a child because we said them every day in school: the Hail Mary, the Glory Be, the Act of Contrition. I then tried to remember the psalm from the Bible that my mom taught me when I was little. "The Lord is my light and my salvation . . ." or something like that.

Was it Psalm 23? Maybe Psalm 27? It was 27, I think. "The Lord is my light and my salvation . . ."

I kept saying that line over and over, dozens of times, until the rest finally came to me: "The Lord is my light and my salvation, whom shall I fear? The Lord is the strength of my life; of whom shall I be afraid?" Yes! That was it! It finally rolled off my tongue. I was so thankful that I could remember it, not only for its meaning and how it applied to my situation, but because it gave me a heart-to-heart connection to my mother—Kathleen Guzman—the strongest, most loving woman I ever knew. She was the primary reason I had any faith at all and—I suddenly realized—someone who might be able to help me out of my predicament.

My relationship with my mom was very open throughout my life. My father was the strict one. Everything was businesslike with him. But with Mom, I felt like I could confide in her about anything. She listened to what I had to say and showed a genuine interest in my thoughts and opinions. Mom was short and pretty; she was a hard-working homemaker who cooked, cleaned, did laundry, took care of all ten of us, and never missed Mass. She also found time, on occasion, to entertain friends and other family members.

Her home was their home. She was an honest, giving person who put everybody else's wants and needs ahead of her own.

In early 1999, Mom visited my sister Celia, who lived in Pennsylvania. It was not only Mom's first time in the United States but her first time on an airplane. She was hesitant to go for that reason, but she did it and was having a wonderful time in the country—until the accident. Mom slipped and fell at Celia's house. She was in some pain, but nothing seemed broken. She went to the hospital for what she figured would be routine treatment, but when doctors took X-rays and ran some tests, they found something that left all of us devastated: Mom had cancer, and it had been growing inside her for a while. It was in her ovaries and her lungs, and the prognosis was bleak. The news was crushing. Mom was only sixty-five years old and the matriarch of the family, the glue that kept us together. For the first time in my life, she appeared vulnerable.

Mom didn't want to be away from home another minute. She immediately flew back to Trinidad to be with my dad and to be examined by her own doctors. They confirmed what the doctors in America found and even went a distressing step further by telling her she only had about six months to live. After sharing the horrible details with the entire family, many of us urged her to go back to the United States, where we felt she would get the best possible treatment and care. But she refused. She wanted to stay in her own country with her husband and children, and die there.

For the next few months, my sisters and I took turns caring for her. I lived forty-five minutes away and generally tended to her at night. My sister Mavis was there for her during the days. On July 4, 1999, a little less than five months after Mom had been diagnosed, most of my family was at her house to spend the weekend with her. I was not going over until the evening because I would be taking care of her that night. As I pulled into the drive, one of my sisters was outside screaming hysterically. A couple of my aunts and brothers were there trying to settle her down. My heart sank into my stomach. I knew exactly what had happened. Kimberly was with me and asked what was wrong. I just looked at her and didn't even have to say anything. She figured it out.

I left her with one of my aunts and raced past everybody into the house. I went into my mother's bedroom and found her in a state I hadn't seen her in since she left for her trip to Pennsylvania: peaceful, in no pain, almost with a smile on her face. I lay down next to my mom and cried, hugging her one last time.

"Good-bye, Mom," I whispered through the tears. "I love you."

CHAPTER TWELVE

Salvation

Two years after my mother's death, here I was, fighting for my life, just as she'd had to fight for hers. The difference was that my mother had died with a clear conscience, knowing she spent her entire life serving my father, her children, her family, her friends, and, most important, the Lord. I continued to pray, this time to my mom. I recited that psalm several times while also asking her if there was anything she could do to get God's attention for me. Anything she could do to help me get out and start my life over. And if not, could she defend me in battle against the devil's desire to take me to his home instead of hers?

I continued praying for what was probably hours, interrupted only by short naps that I just couldn't fight off. I became like a broken record, praying and praying and praying. There was one big problem, though: nothing had changed. I was still stuck, still in pain, and could not hear or feel any type of response from God. I felt in my heart that I had changed, but had I really? Was it enough? I felt like I needed to prove it, but how could I? As time—which felt like an enemy—continued to tick, I got more and more desperate. My praying became infiltrated with a tone of begging and pleading.

"Please, God, I can't take this much longer. Please help me. Don't let me die here. If you can save me, I promise I will live the life that You want. Please hear me. I want to be saved. I will change. I want to see my daughter again. I want to see Roger again."

I was probably rambling, but my heart was on fire. I knew I meant what I was saying, but did He? Did I deserve to be heard? Did I deserve another chance? Was this even about me and what I deserved or about God and His plans? I could grasp somewhere in my brain that I was part of a much bigger picture than my own, but I was unable to escape my own thoughts, my own prayers, my own desires.

I continued imploring God for mercy. The more I spoke to Him, the more I felt that our relationship was gaining some strength. But that wasn't enough. What good does it do to talk to somebody if he or she isn't listening to you? Oh God. Now I had some inkling of how He felt all those years of my life when He was speaking to me but I ignored Him. Was it this painful and disheartening to Him?

"I understand, Lord!" I began to shout. "I really do! Please believe me!" I didn't think I could be broken down any more than I was, but this latest revelation of more of my ignorance was another unflattering layer peeled off me, a layer I was happy to discard. I continued talking to Him with firmness in my voice. It was getting hot again, but I didn't care.

"You HAVE to listen to me!" I shouted as I started to cry. "You have to believe that I will be a different person! I promise, Lord! I promise! I PROMISE!"

I got so emotional that I banged my hand again against the debris that was above my head. When I had done that hours ago, nothing had happened. But this time, it felt and sounded a little loose. I banged harder and harder, screaming louder and louder.

"HELP ME!! LORD, HELP ME!!!" *Bang . . . bang . . . bang . . .* I was breathing heavier, screaming louder, crying harder. "PLEASE GET ME OUT!" *BangBangBangBa . . .*

Suddenly, my hand broke through something above my head. But what did it break through? I still couldn't see any light filtering through. Maybe it was dark out. I tried to look, but couldn't turn my head enough to see. I listened intently, but couldn't hear any noises. Did I just bust through a few inches of a tower's worth of rubble? Was this the devil toying with my mind? I brought my hand down and wiped my eyes to try and see something . . . anything . . . but I couldn't. I put my hand back up there, trying to stretch further. It was an open space, but where did it lead?

Keep praying, Genelle, I reminded myself. *Don't stop praying. Don't fall into the trap of forgetting about God just because you might have made some progress.*

I cried out some more. "Please God. Help me keep going. Help me get out of here. Please hear me! Mom? Are you there? Help me! Help me, please!"

Nothing immediately happened. I continued to pray, continued to feel above my head, and tried to remove more of the debris around the hole. I was running out of physical energy, but never again brought my hand down from that hole. I needed another short nap. I didn't want to take one, but I was so tired. I calmed myself down, grabbed on to the edge of the hole, and closed my eyes. I wouldn't say I slept. It was more like my mind drifted away from where I was, but I was always conscious of my hand staying in that hole. After several minutes, I thought I had begun to hallucinate because I heard sirens and beeping sounds and . . .

"Huh?" I opened my eyes. The sounds . . . they were still there! My eyes were open and the sounds were still there!

"This cannot be a dream," I kept telling myself, as if saying it would help make sure that it wasn't. My heart was racing. Those noises really were sirens, like from fire trucks. And the beeping—that was the sound that a construction truck makes when it's in reverse. I heard it! I heard them all! They were real!

"Oh God, please, this has to be it!" I screamed loudly, or at least as loudly as my dry mouth and throat allowed, which was really probably nothing more than a whimper. I whipped my hand around in the hole, waving it, stretching it as far up as I could.

"I'm down here!" I yelled. "Can you see me? Please help me!"

And that's when I felt it—the warm flesh of another human! He planted his palm firmly against mine and wrapped his long, strong fingers tightly around my hand. I gasped as my breath disappeared momentarily in awe. Was I really feeling this? I was! And all of my hours of asking, praying, screaming, yelling, pleading, begging, promising—they ended with the most incredible feeling and the four sweetest words I have ever heard.

"I've got you, Genelle," a calm, confident male voice said to me. "My name is Paul, and you're going to be okay. They're going to get you out soon."

It was Wednesday, September 12, maybe about 9:15 a.m., nearly twenty-three hours after the tower collapsed.

CHAPTER THIRTEEN

The Other Rescuers

When news of the attacks initially broke the morning of September 11, one man watching it unfold on television at his home, as I later found out, was Rick Cushman. Rick, who was twenty-five years old and in the National Guard, lived in Saugus, Massachusetts, about ten miles north of Boston. Like many heroic people that morning, he felt an obligation, especially given his military background, to use his skills to help. But how?

Once he saw what was happening, he wasted no time, making several phone calls to places such as his National Guard unit and the American Red Cross in his area to see how he could assist, but nobody had any answers for him yet. The towers had just been hit. It was still early, and most organizations were waiting for instructions themselves on what to do. Reluctant to wait,

Rick called Brian Buchanan, a friend of a friend of his who lived nearby and was a former marine. They both agreed they needed to do something and weren't doing anybody any good by sitting at home. Rick had a full-time job at a local restaurant, but his conscience told him he had a much bigger and more important job waiting for him in New York. He changed into his fatigues, tossed a change of clothes or two into the backseat of the car, picked up Brian, and left about noon for the city.

Saugus to New York City is normally about a four-hour drive. On this day, with inbound bridges shut down and traffic at a standstill the closer they got to the city, it took them nearly eight hours to get here. They bailed off the jammed highway at an exit ramp in the Bronx and drove around the streets for a while until they stumbled upon a police station. Looking official in their fatigues, they showed the police their military identifications and, to the men's surprise, were immediately escorted deep into the city. They never expected it to be that easy to get involved, but in a time of crisis and chaos, the police were happy to take any help they could get. Rick followed the police, bumper to bumper, dodging and weaving through some back roads packed with cars and swarming with pedestrians. They went as far as the police felt they could safely take them, which was pretty far—only a handful of blocks from the World Trade Center—when they came upon another police unit that was about to go in even deeper. That new unit told Rick and Brian to follow them and led them almost all the way to Vesey Street, which bordered the towers on the north side. Rick parked his car there, and they walked the rest of the way, right into the rubble. It was pushing 8 p.m. on Tuesday when they stopped at one of the command centers on-site and gazed in awe at their surroundings.

It had been almost ten hours since the towers had collapsed earlier that day, yet an endless trail of floating debris was still gently and hauntingly circling above their heads in the dark, empty sky. The wreckage was a couple of stories high, maybe more in some spots. A shell of the first several stories of one of the sky-scrapers still eerily stood, a stark reminder of what this heap had been earlier in the day.

The two men received their instructions from the command center, which were pretty straightforward: search and rescue. Their mission was to climb atop the rubble and look and listen for any possibility of life. It was still far too early to know just how many people were in and around the buildings when they collapsed. It might have been a few thousand. Some estimates put the number at twenty thousand. Nobody knew for sure. All anybody knew was that it was a lot and that it hadn't happened so long ago that they should give up hope.

They put masks on to help ward off the nauseating smell—a mixture of burning metal, electrical wires, and human flesh. The men knew from what they had seen on television that they were going to be climbing into nothing short of a war zone. They were directed to a smaller building on the site that was heavily damaged but had avoided collapse. They walked inside, cautiously stepping through all the dust and ruins, and up the steps to the second floor. The debris outside the building from the towers was piled so high, and right against the building, that they climbed out a second-story window and found themselves right on top of the mountain of twisted rubble. They had been briefed at the command center on what to expect, but even an explanation in great detail would have never prepared them for this.

They stared incredulously at the endless, perilous wreckage, then warily started walking through the darkness, slowly and carefully stepping across the rough, jagged terrain of peaks and valleys, trying to avoid falling onto some sharp metal that could slice into them. There was also the danger of taking one wrong step and dropping deep into a fiery pit. As they looked down through the rubble, they could see the crimson glow of fires burning, which was also their only real source of light other than a few flashlights and some surrounding city lights. It was like walking on top of a volcano that was waiting to swallow them whole at any moment.

There were four other men in their group, including a couple of New York City firefighters. They didn't have any specific area they were trying to cover. The site was so large and they had to walk so carefully that they weren't going to wander very far anyway. It was all about vigilantly walking, looking, and listening. Search and rescue. That was the sole mission.

They walked among filing cabinets, mangled beams, pipes, desks, chairs, papers, cables, wires, and, sadly, bodies. More parts than whole bodies. Rick says when they found what was once human life, they immediately called the command center, and a crew would come in and carefully place the remains in a bag. The crew would label the bag with any information they could, such as the time found, and the approximate area in which the remains were located—anything that could possibly help authorities later identify the person.

About the only good news, which provided some hope for their mission, was that a couple of people had miraculously been found alive in other parts of the wreckage on that Tuesday night— Port Authority officers John McLoughlin and Will Jimeno, who had been in the South Tower when it collapsed—and were eventually freed several hours later.

The military men from Saugus hoped to be as fortunate in their search.

After working into the wee hours of Wednesday morning, September 12, they both climbed down from the mountain the same way they had gotten up and walked away from the site to give themselves a brief physical and mental rest. They felt they had combed the area as best they could in the short time they had been there and, though unsuccessful in finding anybody alive, still planned to give it another shot a few hours later at daybreak. They walked a few blocks away and found a couple of park benches next to a nearby marina where they slept for maybe two hours. They were awakened by the sunrise, the most depressing sunrise they had ever witnessed. Though shining brightly in the sky, it was shadowed on the ground by a dense, dark vapor that was difficult to see through and breathe in. It was like a dirty eclipse that left no doubt something inhuman had happened in one of the greatest cities in the world and wasn't going to get better anytime soon. But they, like dozens of others who had arrived in town to help, were not about to give up.

The two men stretched some of the soreness and kinks out of their bodies, gathered their thoughts, and walked back to the command center as refreshed as two guys who had gotten a couple of hours of sleep on park benches could be. They picked up some new masks and headed back to the top of the pile through the same building, hoping for a more successful venture.

Joining them in the search in their area that morning was a police officer from Canada named James Symington, who was accompanied by Trakr, his seven-year-old German shepherd. James was from Halifax, Nova Scotia. Trakr was a police and search-and-rescue dog, born in the Czech Republic. He had been owned by the Halifax Regional Police Department but was recently retired and was now James's dog. Trakr's incredible nose had sniffed out hundreds of missing people and millions of dollars in missing goods throughout his career. He was trained to do exactly what search-and-rescue teams needed at the World Trade Center site. When James heard about the attacks, he and Trakr jumped into their car and made what was normally about a seventeen-hour drive to New York in roughly fourteen hours. They went through various checkpoints when they arrived Tuesday night, about the same time Rick and Brian did. They were immediately deployed to the site with several firefighters, who had lost some comrades; the firefighters hoped Trakr could help find some of them still alive.

The officer and his dog worked tirelessly throughout Tuesday evening and into very early Wednesday morning without any success—until about roughly 9:15 a.m. That was when, with Rick and Brian nearby, Trakr came to a sudden stop. James looked down at him and intently watched as Trakr's body became still and erect. That was the first sign that he might be onto something. The German shepherd then started anxiously dancing around. Something was triggering this excitement in him. James, with a firm hold of Trakr's leash, continued to quietly watch as Trakr keenly scoped the area with his eyes. Then came two more signs James was hoping to see: Trakr's ears perked up and his tail stiffened. There was no doubt about it at that point: Trakr sensed somebody close by was buried alive.

That somebody was me.

Exactly where was not clear to them yet, but I was close enough that my smell sent clear messages through Trakr's system. False alarms were always possible, but Trakr had a record of being one of the best there was, and nobody knew him better than James.

James completely trusted his partner's senses and confidently yelled out to the team around him:

"He's got a hit!"

Trakr's "hit," as I would eventually learn, came almost at the exact same time that Paul grabbed my hand.

CHAPTER FOURTEEN

Paul

While Trakr's nose was onto me, I clung to Paul's hand like I was dangling over the side of a ten-thousand-foot-high cliff. I can't imagine I had much strength left, but I felt like I had gripped his hand so tightly I might break it. It felt as if we couldn't have been pried apart with a crowbar. My eyes were opened, but I still couldn't see anything. I tried to peer through where the hole was, but still saw only solid darkness. I wasn't sure how it was possible to not be able to see even a glimmer of light with someone on the other end holding my hand, but as long as I could feel Paul's hand and hear his voice, I was happy.

"Please don't let go, Paul," I said with a tone of desperation.

"Don't worry, I've got you," he replied, sounding cool and collected. "I'm not going anywhere until help arrives. They're almost here. I can see them."

"Thank you, Paul!" I cried. "Thank you! Thank you! Oh, God, thank you!"

I had no idea at the time who the "help" was that Paul was talking about, though I learned later that it included James, Trakr, Rick, and Brian. I don't remember hearing Paul communicate with them, or asking Paul who was coming, or how far away they were, because I really didn't need specifics. Just knowing how fortunate I was that somebody had found me and that people were on their way to get me out was exhilarating. As securely as my hand was in Paul's, I had to continue to trust that my fate was truly in God's hands and that He was going to take care of everything the way He saw fit.

As I held on to Paul, the pain throughout my body ceased. No head throbbing, no pain in my legs. Or maybe it hadn't really gone away at all, but I was just too elated to care or think about it.

"Can you see anybody coming yet?" I anxiously asked.

"They're almost here," Paul said. I still didn't press him for details of what he could see. My throat hurt a lot, so I didn't feel like talking any more than I had to. I'd waited blindly for this long—what was a few more minutes going to matter?

While Paul was holding my hand, James and Trakr, as I later learned, continued on to another section of debris to search for other signs of life, but Rick, Brian, and other searchers stayed in my general area, hoping to visually or audibly pick up on what Trakr had smelled. Their search went on for a few minutes. Finally, at about 9:30 a.m., Rick spotted something under a pile of rubble. It was barely visible, but it caught his attention because of its fluorescent orange color. He walked closer to make sure he was seeing what he thought he was seeing. He was hoping he was wrong . . . but sadly, he was pretty certain he wasn't.

It appeared to be the dead body of a New York City firefighter. Rick knew that the unwritten rule and show of respect in a situation like that was to immediately call another firefighter over to allow him to get his brother. With a fireman standing nearby, that's what Rick did.

Meanwhile, my arm was getting very tired. It didn't feel like Paul's grip had loosened a bit, so I let some of the tension out of my arm and hand and let him do all the work holding it up.

"How close are they?" I asked him.

"They're just about here," Paul said. It was true, I learned later, that the fireman that Rick had called over was getting much closer—closer to the deceased fireman . . . and at the same time, closer to Paul and me. Rick and Brian stood in the vicinity, watching as the fireman approached the body.

When he got to it, he knelt down and carefully scraped away some of the dust and debris to get a closer look, to verify that it was one of his own. It was. He stayed on his knee and paused for a moment in sorrow. Little did he know that by finding his comrade, he would be part of a miracle that had been slowly unfolding since the towers collapsed.

After his short reflection, he looked down closer, and then listened attentively before turning his head to the other rescuers in the area.

"Hey! We've got a live person here!" the fireman shouted. Everybody froze. Voices went dead silent. You could have heard a pin drop. That's how quiet it was. It stayed that way for several seconds. The fireman then turned back to the rubble and waved his flashlight in the area around his deceased brother.

"Can you see the light?" he shouted to the live person he found.

That person was me.

"No, I can't see anything," I yelled back.

Meanwhile, Paul was still holding my hand.

"Hang on, Genelle," Paul said. "They'll get you."

All the rescue workers in the area, responding to the fireman's call that he found a live person, unfroze as they migrated as quickly and carefully as they could over to me. I could hear what sounded like dozens of feet pounding on the rubble above me.

"I'm down here!" I yelled with a hoarse voice. "Can you see me?"

But wait a minute . . . I was still holding on to Paul's hand. What was going on? Why wasn't Paul communicating with the rescuers? He said earlier that he could see them. Couldn't they see him too? My hand was becoming a little numb from not moving it for so long. I wiggled my fingers around Paul's hand, just to reassure myself that he was still holding on to me.

"Paul, what's happening?" I frantically asked, trying to make sense of the situation.

"You're okay, Genelle," he said in the same composed tone he'd been speaking in since he'd found me about twenty minutes earlier. "One more minute and they'll have you."

"I can't believe this is happening," I cried. I was so confused about what was going on above me. I had Paul talking to me, the fireman talking to me, but they weren't talking to each other. I didn't have the mental strength to try and figure it out. All that mattered to me at that moment was that several people knew where I was, including one who had a solid grip on me.

"Keep the faith, Genelle," I mumbled to myself. "Trust God. Trust . . ."

Suddenly, some of the debris above me started to move. I shut my eyes and mouth as particles of dust fell onto me.

"Careful," I could hear a couple of men telling each other. "Eeeasy. Eeeasy."

More dust came raining down as the noise of moving debris got louder. Suddenly, a stream of bright sunlight cracked through, forcing me to keep my eyes firmly closed. I tried to open them, but they were too caked in soot, and it was way too bright after having been in total darkness for so long.

"Paul? Paul?" I said, spitting some dust off my lips.

"They're here, Genelle," Paul said in a voice that I could tell was accompanied with a smile. "They're here."

"Oh God, thank you, Paul! Thank you!"

"You're in good hands now," he said. "I'm going to go and let them do their jobs and get you out, okay?"

"Okay. Thank you."

I really didn't know how to express my gratitude. I kept saying his name to myself in my head after he left so that I wouldn't forget it. I wanted to make sure I found him and thanked him in the coming days. Meanwhile, the fireman who found me held my hand just as Paul did.

In fact, I couldn't even remember Paul's letting go and the fireman's taking over. It was a heavenly transition.

"What's your name?" he said with a sound of pure joy in his voice.

"Genelle," I said softly, overwhelmed with relief.

"It's going to take us awhile, Genelle," he said, "but we will get you out of here."

His fellow fireman, whom he had originally come over to get, was lying under me and behind me, part of him crushed underneath my legs. Remember that soft cloth I felt behind my legs after the tower first collapsed? The one I later tugged at when I was freezing, unaware of what it was, but hoping to pull it over me to keep warm? That was the uniform—with the fluorescent orange glow that Rick spotted—of the fireman.

CHAPTER FIFTEEN

Freedom

I can't begin to guess how many people surrounded me. I still couldn't open my eyes, but it sounded like there were fifty voices talking at once, all filled with urgency and excitement. It was a nonstop loop of "move this" and "move that" and "don't move this" and "don't move that." Every time one person began to do something, a dozen more would jump in with their opinions of how it should or should not be done. It was quite a scintillating experience, especially with my eyes closed, because the sounds were all that I was focused on. The rescuers were working in full cooperation with one another, all with one goal: to get me out safely. While they were working on freeing me, Rick and Brian had backed off and moved on in the same direction as James and Trakr to look for other survivors. Finding me gave them hope that there could be more, and they figured it was best to leave my physical rescue to the professionals.

"There's going to be a lot of sawing and cutting going on around you," the fireman said as he continued to hold my hand. "You'll be fine, but it's going to be pretty noisy."

"Okay," I said, happy to oblige with whatever anybody told me. I can't say that the thought of saws buzzing around my head and extremities was comforting, but these were God's men, in my mind. Just as I had put all my trust in Him to get me out, I had to trust that He sent these men to finish the job. But the fireman wasn't kidding about the noise. There was constant clanging and grinding all around me from their tools and equipment. Each tool or piece of machinery had its own distinct sound, none of which would be pleasant to the average ear. To me, though, they were the beautiful sounds of freedom in the making. Every grind, every bang, every ring meant I was that much closer to being out. I don't know specifically what they used, but it sounded like circular saws, jackhammers, and blowtorches, to name a few. As much as I wanted to open my eyes, I think it was better that I couldn't. Had I been able to see the sharp steel blades spinning or orange sparks flying around my head, it probably would have been tough to stomach.

They began working on freeing my head, chipping away at the solid, heavy concrete a little bit to lighten it. That went on for several minutes. When they were finally able to pick it up and toss it all aside, it felt like my head instantly ballooned about five sizes larger than it was supposed to be. I probably wasn't a very pretty sight, but for the first time in my life, I didn't care what I looked like. It was a relief to have that pressure eliminated. I felt like I could breathe easier, and feeling the outdoor air—as dirty as it was—brushing against my forehead was something I never thought I would be so grateful for.

"You doing okay, Genelle?" the fireman asked.

"Absolutely," I replied with a smile.

"Can you tell me where you were before you ended up down here?"

I took a deep breath and thought about it for a minute.

"We were on the thirteenth floor coming down the stairs . . ." I went through the whole story of our trying to escape down the stairwell, then backtracked to when it all started—the sound of breaking glass, the shaking, the swaying, the panic, seeing the buildings on television, Rosa . . . oh Rosa.

"My friend Rosa was holding my hand down the stairs, then let go as the building was coming down. Do you know . . . ?"

I stopped myself. I was afraid of what his answer would be to what I felt was a futile question.

"I don't know if she made it or not," the fireman said bluntly, "but people are still searching right now, and we're going to continue searching as soon as we get you out. We found you, so we're not giving up on anybody."

That put a smile back on my face. I don't know if I really believed that Rosa, Susan, Pasquale, or anybody else in our group would be found alive, but he was right. If I was alive, and with God's presence, there was always hope.

The rescue effort continued as several of the men talked to me throughout the process. They told me when they were moving to another part of my body, I guess so that I wasn't startled if I felt something, and so that I would keep still, though that wasn't a problem. I'm sure they were also trying to keep me engaged so I would stay awake and stay positive. I obviously needed medical attention, but they didn't know how seriously I needed it, and it couldn't be administered until they first got me out.

After freeing my head, they worked their way down to my midsection. They lifted my upper body slightly, enough to gently pull my right arm out from underneath me. I felt about a dozen hands on me at once. Each move was done very slowly and meticulously. They had no idea what was broken and seemed to be working with the assumption that everything on me was damaged in some way. That overly cautious approach was perfectly acceptable to me.

Once my arm was free, they set me back down and gave me some time to try and move a little bit and get the blood flowing while they discussed what to do next and how to do it. I tenderly turned my head to the left, feeling every joint in my neck pop as I did. I tried to wiggle the fingers on my right hand and bend my elbow. I think it felt like I was moving them more than I actually was, but just knowing that I now had the capability to try and move them was a relief. Everything was sore, unlike any soreness I'd ever felt, but I wasn't complaining.

Now able to turn my head a little bit, I asked the fireman for some water. Much to my shock, he would not give me any. He wanted to, because he could tell by my voice how dry my throat was, but I think he also realized that I probably inhaled and swallowed a lot of dust and other pollutants. What harm drinking water on top of that would have done, I don't know. Maybe it would have done more damage. Whatever the case, I know he was just being cautious, and I totally trusted his judgment.

"We'll get you some after we get you out of here," he said.

With my head and right arm now free, the rescuers turned their attention to freeing my legs, the most difficult and time-consuming part of the rescue. It seemed as if they spent an hour or two just cutting away the beam that was holding my legs down, mainly because there were so many obstacles hindering their efforts. I think, from listening to what they were saying, the beam was buried on each end. To try and unbury it so they could lift it out not only would have taken an inordinate amount of time, but would have made the entire situation more dangerous. The fireman told me at one point that we were positioned on a very high pile of rubble, and there was no telling how secure everything was beneath us. There was also the issue of my body, along with that of the dead fireman. My legs were crushed directly by the beam, so the rescuers had to be careful how deep they cut into the steel. The fireman's body was right under my legs, and they needed to be respectful of that. I could hear a blowtorch going on and off and could feel the heat from it each time it was on.

"He's a professional, Genelle," the fireman told me, as if he were sensing my trepidation.

"I know," I said. I was growing very tired, but it seemed like every time my mind started to wander, I was quickly yanked out of my trance with "Be careful! Be careful!" Those were the words I heard the most throughout the whole ordeal. I bet they said them a hundred times since they started, and every time, thank God, they listened to one another.

I could tell when the beam was finally lifted off me only because I could feel the air on my left leg. But I could hardly move it, and the right one just felt like it was dead. I couldn't move it.

I couldn't feel it. If they had told me it wasn't there, I would have believed them. But I wasn't too worried about it at that point. I was alive and knew I was going to have a long road to recovery ahead of me. First things first—just get me out.

The entire process took about three and a half to four hours. I think it was about 1:30 p.m. when they were finally ready to lift me out. I had been buried underneath that rubble for about twenty-three hours when they found me, and it was roughly twenty-seven hours before I was freed. How on earth did I survive being crushed by one of the most massive structures on the planet? How did I last as long as I did in those conditions? The change that was transpiring in me made those questions easy to answer. I didn't do any of it. It was all God. He had a plan for me—one I could neither explain nor take an ounce of credit for. But I firmly believe that the first of countless steps in His plan for me was to draw me near to Him.

I apologized, and He accepted. I promised, and He believed. At least that is what I now believed. It didn't feel like only concrete and beams had been lifted off me, but a dark veil that had been shrouding me for years as well. It was a wonderful, magical feeling to know that the best story I was going to have to tell from my tribulation to my family and friends was that, when it was over, I had made a new best friend, one I could count on for anything and one I would spend the rest of my life serving with honor and glory.

Once everything around me was cleared away, they brought in a rescue basket to carry me out. It was basically a stretcher, but with a short wall encircling it to prevent me from falling out. They lowered it next to me and gently lifted me. Keeping me as low to the ground as possible, they practically slid me into the basket. Once I was in, I was securely strapped across the upper, mid, and lower sections of my body. But their work was far from over. While the biggest challenge for the rescuers was getting me out of the hole, they now had to get me to the ambulance several yards away. I had been buried under probably just a few feet of rubble, if that, but was on top of much more: twenty, maybe thirty feet, is what I heard some people say. So, somehow, they had to carry me down that far without dropping me or hurting themselves. Had it been a smooth road, it would have been easy. But there was no rhyme or reason to the terrain we were on. One step might be some jagged metal. The next step might be sharp or slick glass. The next might require stepping over a beam. The next could drop us into a hole. For a group of people to navigate that together, all the while carrying a body in a basket, was precarious work. But leave it to the smart, hard-working, creative New Yorkers to quickly figure out how to do it.

While I was being dug out, dozens and dozens of volunteers in the vicinity flocked to the scene, ready to do whatever necessary to transport me to the waiting ambulance. And when I say "dozens and dozens," I've been told there were at least two hundred, and probably even closer to three hundred. Simply unfathomable to me. They formed two lines. Separated a few feet apart, they faced each other, basically forming a human tunnel. They stood outside the hole I was in and snaked all the way down the rubble to the ambulance.

"You ready, Genelle?" one of them said.

I couldn't have smiled any brighter. "Absolutely," I replied. The fireman who had been at my side gave my hand one more squeeze.

"You did good," he said.

"Thank you for everything," I said, unsure of how to thank a man who played a major role in saving my life. I still could barely open my eyes, so I had no idea what he looked like. And I realized just a few seconds after thanking him that throughout the entire rescue, he never told me his name. How did I not ask? But it was already too late. The split second after saying "Thank you for everything," my descent down the heap of rubble had begun.

With my head pointing in the direction of the ambulance, I was off . . . and never did I expect it to be the physical ride that it was. The saws and hammers and blowtorches that had cut and chipped and burned the concrete and metal around me were more pleasant than that ride in the basket. The two lines of helpers could not stand shoulder-to-shoulder evenly, nor could they necessarily stand on the same level as those across from them. As they passed me down the line, like a crowd surfer at a rock concert, I went downhill, uphill, side to side, oftentimes feeling like I might flip over. I was bouncing out of control. When I opened my eyes very slightly, I still couldn't see much, which gave me the sensation of riding a roller coaster in the dark. I had no idea how far along I was at any point in my journey, and it seemed to go on forever and ever. I was starting to wonder if they were just going to pass me all the way to the hospital.

Trust me—I wasn't complaining. Whatever it took to get me to the ambulance was okay with me, but it was just not something I was ready for.

Mentally, though, the ride was uplifting. Everybody commented while they passed me along. I heard "hang in there" and "way to go" and "God bless you" and dozens of other such phrases of encouragement. I occasionally opened my eyes to try and catch a glimpse of some of these folks. I was barely able to see, so I mainly just smiled with my eyes closed and tried to enjoy my journey to freedom.

Once I reached the end of the line, I was startled by their roaring cheers. They erupted into applause, as if we were at a sold-out Yankees game. It was an amazing, beautiful sound. But were those cheers for me? I hoped it was for all of them—the brave men and women who left their spouses and children and jobs to risk their lives to find lost souls such as me. I will forever be indebted to them. They are my heroes.

As the cheering faded, I was loaded into the back of an ambulance and the doors were closed. One medical technician immediately sprayed my eyes with some kind of fluid, which cleaned them out and enabled me to open them more. Another medic put a tube down my throat for a couple of minutes that made me gag. I assume it was something to help clear out my lungs. Once the tube was removed, I relaxed as a smile spread naturally across my face again. The driver flipped the siren on and we sped off to Bellevue Hospital Center.

"Are you taking me home?" I asked. Compared to where I had been for the previous day, I was feeling like a million bucks.

"No," one of the technicians laughed. "You're going straight to the hospital."

The ambulance was flying. I don't know how fast we were going, but it felt as fast as probably any vehicle had ever gone through the typically gridlocked city. It didn't take long to reach our destination, but I'll never forget my thoughts as we drove. I thought about all that I had been through in just one day. It was amazing to me that I could go thirty years with the influence of God all around me—from my parents, from Elvis, from many relatives, from church, from school, even from Kimberly—and never feel much of any allegiance or debt to Him. Yet here I was transformed in a single day. The best part was that I knew this wasn't a one-time call to Him. It was no fluke. I knew without a doubt that this was the beginning of something big, a relationship that was going to be the focal point of the rest of my life.

As we approached the hospital, I thought some more about Paul. I wasn't able to see the wreckage as they carried me away, but with more than a hundred floors, and for as far as I traveled in that stretcher to get to the ambulance, it had to be massive. There was no way it was coincidence that Paul found me. Just no way. God led him there. But why me? There had to be so many other people more worthy than I, based on the good lives they led, of being saved. Maybe I had some kind of previous connection to Paul that I didn't know about. But still, how did he find me buried under there? Who was he? A fireman? A policeman? An everyday citizen just there to help? I thought about the path he might have taken to find me. From being at home with his family to being on site of one of the worst disasters in the nation's history. He probably climbed around the pile for hours, digging, yelling, listening, searching for any sign of life. Did he find anybody before me? After he let go of my hand, did he continue searching for more? And did he find anybody?

I had a million questions about him and for him that I knew wouldn't be answered until I got out of the hospital and was able to track him down. What type of life had Paul led? Was finding me a life-changing experience for him? Or was this routine for him, just another day's work, something he did for a living?

In short, who was this man who, through God's grace, had become my hero? Who was this man whose selflessness gave me, of all people, a second chance at life? I couldn't wait to meet him and find out.

CHAPTER SIXTEEN

Pillars of Strength

As I was being checked in to Bellevue Hospital, Roger was back at our apartment, trying to recover from his hangover. He woke up sometime around 9:30 a.m. on Wednesday—right about the time I was found—hoping that the previous day had been a nightmare. But the empty bottle of rum lying on the bed, along with his heavy, throbbing head, indubitably reminded him that every bit of it was real. He continued to pray out loud right where he left off the previous night, asking God to tell him what he needed to do to bring me back, before he despondently gave up, at least for the moment.

He sluggishly wandered into the living room where Camille was watching television. Carla, my niece, was also there, as was Esther, an old friend of Roger's and mine from Trinidad. Corey had also spent the night but had already left for work.

"Morning," Roger mumbled.

"How you feeling?" Camille somberly replied.

"All right," he muttered as his pounding skull told him otherwise. Just a minute or two of seeing the images and hearing the reporters on television talk about what happened Tuesday was enough to make him turn right back around and retreat to the bedroom.

"Thanks for being here," he said to all of them, "but I'm just not going to be very good company right now." He lay back down in bed and closed his eyes, continuing to pray again, but depressing thoughts were overshadowing his desperate prayers.

The thoughts were only making his head hurt more, but they were beyond his control. He had a sliver of hope, maybe 10 percent, he says, that I was still alive, but that was only because he hadn't received official confirmation yet that I was dead. He knew the reality of the situation. He stood alone outside the North Tower, waiting for me long after I should have been out. He watched one tower fall, and then heard the other one fall. He witnessed the injured, the bloodied, the dead. He saw people running out of the buildings for their lives, and I was not one of them. He checked his cell's voice mail. Nothing.

Roger rolled in and out of consciousness for several hours, trying to stay awake and pray, but often succumbed to the grief and physical pain. It was roughly 3 p.m., maybe 3:30, when the phone in his apartment rang. It had been ringing a lot throughout the morning and early afternoon as people called to check on him and see if there had been any more news about me. He let Camille answer them all, as she did this most recent call. After hanging up, Camille rushed down the hall to Roger's bedroom and knocked on the door.

"Roger?"

"Hmm?"

"Can I come in?"

"Yes."

Camille walked in to find him stretched out on top of the covers with his eyes closed.

"Roger, that was Bellevue Hospital on the phone."

He didn't move for about three stunned seconds as he processed what she said, then opened his eyes and popped his head up.

"What did they say?" he asked.

"They asked if Roger McMillan lived here. I told them you did, that you were sleeping, and they said you need to go down there."

"Why?"

"I asked, but they wouldn't tell me," Camille dolefully said, thinking the same thing that immediately popped into Roger's mind—that my body had been found. "They said they need to talk to you." Roger laid his head back down and stared straight up at the ceiling.

"There is no way I'm identifying her body," he said as tears started to fill his eyes. "I can't do it. I can't see her that way."

"We don't know that's the case, Roger. Let's just go and find out." She left the bedroom to let Roger get dressed.

After a few minutes, he came out. The three ladies, his three pillars of support that day, gave him hugs before they all headed out the door together. They were fortunate, with much of the transportation system in chaos, to catch a train, and then a bus, into Manhattan. It took nearly ninety minutes, but mentally it felt like the longest ride of Roger's life.

"I can't look at her if she's dead," Roger reiterated on the train.

"I just can't." Saying that out loud again made him remember that Corey had a friend who worked at Bellevue. Roger wasn't sure what that friend's job was, but he was hoping she was someone who could shed some light on the mysterious phone call he got from the hospital. He dialed Corey's cell phone.

"Corey? Hey, I'm heading into town with Camille, Carla, and Esther. Bellevue called and said I needed to go in there."

"What for?"

"I have no idea. Camille took the call, and they wouldn't tell her. They just said Roger McMillan needs to come in. That's why I'm calling you. Does your friend still work there?"

"Yeah, yeah, absolutely," Corey said.

"Do you think she can see what she can find out? If they're calling me in to identify Genelle's body, I'm not doing it. I can't."

"Yeah, sure, let me try to call her and I'll call you right back."

"Okay, thanks."

Roger hung up, and the long journey continued. They transferred from the train to the bus. That got them as close to the hospital as possible, but still left them several blocks away, forcing them to walk. Just as they were beginning their trek, Roger's phone rang. It was Corey, who was holding the answer to the question Roger had been wanting to know since Bellevue first called: was I dead or alive?

Think about what horrible news you could possibly receive that would sink your soul to the bottom of the ocean, then imagine what could be the best news you could get that would shoot it to the stars. Now imagine emotionally blasting from the ocean floor to the sky in a heartbeat. That's what happened to Roger. After being convinced that I was gone forever . . .

"Roger? It's Corey. She's alive!"

Roger's heartbeat kicked uncontrollably into high gear.

"She's . . . what?"

"She's alive, Roger! She's at Bellevue!"

"Oh, praise God! She's alive!" Roger said to the ladies, who erupted in celebration.

"Hey, Roger," Corey yelled through the phone, trying to recapture his brother's attention. "There's one thing though that my friend warned me about."

"What's that?"

"She's not going to look like the Genelle you know. Her entire face and head is very swollen. She's pretty banged up right now. She's going to make it, but she's been through a lot. So be prepared for that before you go in there."

"Okay," Roger said. "Thanks, brother. I'll call you a little later."

Roger told the ladies what Corey said about my appearance. They tried to imagine just how bad I could possibly look . . . but then realized they didn't care. I was alive, and that's all that mattered. Everything else was secondary.

They all made calls from their cell phones while continuing their walk, which now felt like a victory parade rather than a funeral procession. They called every family member and friend they could think of, and word quickly spread to Trinidad . . . and to Kimberly.

Kimberly, like Roger, had very little doubt in her mind that I was dead. After talking with her dad about it for a while Tuesday night, trying to make sense of it the best that a twelve-year-old could, she cried herself to sleep, asking God the same questions Roger was asking and the same ones I had been asking while I was under the rubble: would God give me another chance to live? Come to think of it, God was probably being assailed with prayers at the exact same time by Roger, Kimberly, and me, not to mention all the family and friends who were praying. That thought later made me recall the miracle I believe I witnessed years earlier involving my aunt Hilda and how I credited that, in part, to all the people surrounding her in prayer. I felt my situation was different when I was praying for a miracle because I didn't have all those people physically gathered around me. I felt like I was alone and on my own. But even though I could not see them, there were people praying just as hard, and in large numbers, for my survival. I felt like I was alone at the time, but I never was. Not even close.

When Kimberly woke up on Wednesday, she continued to pray, but was in no mood to go to school. Word was spreading quickly among her friends that I was missing, and, actually, it was spreading all across the island as my name was being tossed around on the television and radio news. I was becoming famous in my native land, as I had always dreamed but for all the wrong reasons.

It was soon after Roger and the others found out from Corey that I was alive that Kimberly and Elvis got the call at home from my sister Christine. Kimberly shrieked with excitement at the news from her aunt.

"Can I talk to her?" were the first words out of my baby's mouth.

"Roger is not even at the hospital yet, honey," Christine said. "But he's on his way and will make sure you get to talk to her as soon as possible."

"Please ask them to tell her I love her," Kimberly said.

When Roger and the others arrived at the hospital, they

checked in and found seats in the crowded lobby. It was crammed wall-to-wall with people, many looking like they had been crying for hours. Everybody either remained silent or talked quietly within his or her own group, simply out of respect for others. Nobody knew who was there for what reason. Some may have been relatives of victims with slight injuries. Others may have been related to someone who was barely hanging on to life. For Roger—he had no idea what my condition was but was about to find out.

"Roger McMillan," a staff member called out. Roger jumped out of his chair.

"Can they come with me?" Roger asked, pointing to Camille, Carla, and Esther.

"I'm sorry," she replied. "Just one person."

Roger hugged the ladies before heading to my room. On their way up, the staffer gave him a gown and mask to wear. As they got to the room, the woman reiterated what Corey had told Roger earlier: I was not going to look like the person he was used to seeing. Roger nodded his head. He didn't care. He just wanted to see me.

With Roger's heart beating excitedly, they entered the room. It was quiet, except for some beeping monitors, and was very dimly lit. Roger walked over to my bedside and looked at me. And he looked. And he looked. Then he turned and looked at the lady with bewilderment. Then he looked back at me. And continued looking. His heart was sinking. All of that joy of seeing me and now . . . they had the wrong person? Roger skeptically moved closer. All he could see was someone with a very swollen head, covered completely in white dust—the hair, the face, the arms— all white.

"Genelle?" he said dubiously. I had a suction tube in my mouth and down my throat that was extracting contaminants I had inhaled, preventing me from talking. I lifted my left arm a little bit off the bed and slowly waved my hand. He hesitantly took it, and I squeezed as hard as I could.

"Genelle?" he said again.

I squeezed his hand some more. That's when he knew for sure it was me. He smiled with relief, then tenderly whispered words that I will never forget:

"Why didn't you get out when I told you to?"

I smiled, or at least I felt like I was smiling, as a single joy-filled teardrop flowed from my left eye and streamed down my cheek. Roger gently wiped it away as he began to cry with me.

"Oh, Genelle," he said. "Thank God you're here. Thank God."

CHAPTER SEVENTEEN

Healing

It was the next day, I believe—right after the tube had been removed from my throat—when the phone in my room rang. Roger answered it.

"It's for you," he said, handing the receiver to me. I was feeling pretty weak and not much in the mood to talk, but I knew he wouldn't have handed it to me if it hadn't been somebody important.

"Hello?" I said.

"Mom?"

"Kimberly!" I took a deep breath, then started to cry. "My baby—how are you?" I couldn't believe I was talking to her. I was trying to listen to her while thanking God in my head at the same time.

"I'm good," she said. She sounded different—more mature. "How are you?"

"Well, I've been better," I said with a chuckle, wiping away the tears with my free hand. "But I could be a lot worse."

We didn't talk for too long, given my condition and the distance of the call, but just to hear her voice made it worthwhile. She asked me what happened, and I told her as succinctly and with as few details as possible. That just wasn't the time or place to go deeply into it. She briefly told me what she went through before finding out I was alive. It was a very emotional, personal conversation with some crying, smiling, and a lot of love back and forth. She said she wanted to visit me, but I told her I was okay and it was best if she stayed home. I didn't want her missing any school, and I also didn't want her seeing me in such bad shape. Plus, I didn't know if New York was still being targeted by terrorists, if there was more danger to come. Of course, I hoped not, but I wasn't ready to take my chances by bringing my daughter to the city. And I certainly didn't want her flying alone on an airplane.

I told her we'd be together soon enough, and that we would continue talking a lot more in the days to come. I got the feeling she felt like she got her mom back—the mom she always wanted—and I knew that she did.

"I love you, Mom," she said as we concluded our conversation. I began to cry again.

"I love you, too, baby."

And then there was Roger, the one constant in the hospital every day during the six weeks I was there. He would wake up in our apartment by himself at the crack of dawn, ride the train into town, go straight to the hospital, and sit by my side all day long. He would make sure I was comfortable, help me eat, read the Bible to me, help me with my rehabilitation. And on days when he had to work, he would only go in for about a half day, then come over to the hospital. He didn't leave my side until about 11 p.m. It had to have taken a physical and mental toll on him, but he never complained, never acted like he didn't want to be there, and always did everything he could for me. It was truly a blessing on our relationship because it showed that even through bad times, he was going to be there for me. I never doubted that, but to see it in action was wonderful.

Other than his steadfast presence each day, what happened those six weeks was a whirlwind—the visits from friends and family, the phone calls, the nurses constantly checking on me, the surgeries, the diagnoses I never expected, the physical therapy, the immigration issue—I cannot even remember the order in which everything happened because there was so much going on; there was certainly never a dull moment.

On the physical side, a day or two after I was there, nurses were finally able to clean me up a little bit. The swelling went down with time, and I started to look a little bit like the person I used to be. My health issues were pretty clear cut at that point. My eyes were fine, and my lungs were okay. I had some scrapes, mainly on my back and arms and had to have some stitches in three different places on my left leg. The biggest damage was to my right leg, which had been pinned under me. The doctors gave it to me straight: there were some broken bones, along with dam-aged nerves and muscles from my thigh down through my foot; I was probably going to have to go through multiple surgeries over the next few weeks, and amputation of the leg was not out of the question.

My reaction to the amputation possibility? Believe it or not, it was "Whatever." That was probably my first real test since I was found alive that I had completely put my life in God's hands. No, I did not want to lose my leg, but if that was the worst thing that was going to happen to me after experiencing what I had experienced, I was fine with it. God kept me alive for a reason, and the loss of a leg wasn't going to change that.

The first surgery took place within the first few days, and my leg was immediately put in a cast to keep it immobilized. The second and third surgeries were performed soon after, and the leg was again put in a cast each time. The doctors didn't tell me a whole lot after each of the first two surgeries other than to say that they had gone as expected. But after the third surgery, the news was a little grimmer.

"The leg is dead," was the doctor's blunt admission. "We're going to try one more surgery to see what we can do, but we just don't know for sure how it's going to turn out."

I guess you could say I passed my second test after that news. While the thought of losing my leg became a little more real, I was still okay with it. It felt as if nothing could dampen my joy of surviving.

The surgery they performed was called a fasciotomy, in which the fascia, or connective tissue surrounding the muscles and nerves in the damaged area, was cut to relieve some pressure. A lot of tissue was also removed, so much that it left a permanent indentation in my leg, and the surgery left some scars on the left and right sides of that leg. But the surgery was successful. About the worst news I got was that wearing miniskirts probably wouldn't be so attractive anymore. They saved my dead leg and saw no reason for me not to make a full recovery.

After that fourth surgery, I was on crutches and began my physical therapy. It was a painful process but was going pretty well with my mobility continually improving. I was feeling good, like I was making progress each day—until I suffered a major setback.

As I was doing my workout with the therapists one morning, I fainted. I had been feeling a little light-headed just before I passed out but didn't really think much of it. I just figured it was from the exertion of my therapy and came with the territory of rehabbing. The nurses woke me up and took me back to my room.

"We'll try again tomorrow," one of the nurses told me. "You just relax today."

That was the first time I'd ever fainted in my life. It reminded me of a time earlier in the year when I was riding the train into work and felt like I might pass out but didn't. I didn't think much of it then either.

I went back to therapy the next day and gave it another go, making sure I ate something before I went—but it happened again. I just stopped in the middle of my workout and fainted. That's when the doctors and nurses became concerned and decided to give me another break, but this time they ran some tests. They came back soon after with some startling news.

"You have an irregular heartbeat," a cardiologist informed me. He said it could have been congenital and simply didn't pose a problem until now. He didn't seem overly concerned, but I could sense there was more he wanted to tell me.

"What does that mean for me?" I asked, feeling a little bit nervous.

"Well, we're going to run a few more tests," he said. "It's possible that we will have to implant a pacemaker, after which you can go about your normal life. But we'll see how the tests come out."

If I needed a pacemaker, so be it. I just wanted to get it done and get back to my therapy.

After some more tests, they decided to try another option first and put me on some medication to see if that would kick the heart back into gear. The results, thankfully, were immediate; and they decided that a pacemaker was not necessary. I would probably be on this medication for life, they said, but I could certainly live with that.

I was able to continue with therapy, working my leg back to full strength. Well, for a little while, anyway . . . until the next major problem they found.

As if a crushed leg and heart problem weren't enough, nurses did a pap smear after my surgeries. What I thought was just going to be a routine screening drove me to fear when the results came back: signs of cervical cancer. One of the nurses told me that I would likely have to have my uterus removed, meaning, of course, that I would not be able to have any more children. I stared at her in stunned silence, then began to cry. All I can recall is thinking, *Okay, seriously Lord, what's next?* I had been so full of praise, so willing to take whatever bad news came. But cancer? Cancer is life threatening. Could I handle having my life threatened again, so soon after the first event? I wasn't certain how much more I could take. And although we had never formally discussed having children together, I knew Roger wanted children. How would he react to the news?

Much to my relief, Roger remained as calm and loving as ever. "Whatever happens, Genelle, is what was meant to be." I don't know what I would have done without his love and support every step of the way.

I trusted in Roger's word and the next day received some wonderful news. After further evaluation, removing the uterus was not likely going to be necessary. Doctors instead did a LEEP procedure, in which the abnormal cervical cells were basically burned out of me. It took about thirty minutes, and that was it. Follow-up tests showed that the procedure worked and the cancerous cells were gone.

How many times would God save me? I felt so very undeserving of His mercy.

While those physical issues were enough to keep my emotions fluttering all day and every day, they were only a small part of the mental challenges I went through during my hospital stay.

One of the first visits I got was from representatives with the Red Cross, who were there to see what I needed and how they could help. I was appreciative that they took the time to check on me, but when they began asking me for personal information, I started getting nervous. I had kept my immigration status under wraps for so long at work without any problem before 9/11, but I had promised God I would not do that anymore. My status was the furthest thing from my mind until the Red Cross got to the hospital and I realized it might become an issue. It had me wondering about the medical care I would receive. I had insurance through the temp agency, but what was going to happen once they found out I was in the country illegally? Was I going to be kicked out of the hospital? Was I going to be sent back to Trinidad on a stretcher? Fortunately, the Red Cross's questions didn't force me to reveal anything that would signal to them that I was illegal. I still planned to tell someone as I'd promised to God, but this gave me a little more time to prepare.

I decided the person who needed and deserved to know first was my boss from the temp agency, who had been patiently waiting for my paperwork. She came to visit me very soon after the Red Cross left and was so kind, asking me how I was doing and about the care I was getting. I told her it was wonderful.

"But . . ." I hesitated, struggling to find the right words. "The problem is . . ."

That was as far as I got when she interrupted me. I didn't have to say anything more.

"I know," she said with a sympathetic smile. "Don't worry about it. All of your medical care will be taken care of."

I was stunned. Somehow she knew. And somehow she took care of it. I didn't know what to say and really wasn't sure how to feel. I was relieved, because my body was a mess, and there was no doubt I was going to need serious medical attention for a while, but I wasn't expecting any more help at that point. I wasn't legal. Why should I be helped? I had realized by that time how wrong it was to be in the country without permission. Yes, I had come to America to work hard and make a better life for my daughter and me, but it didn't mean I could circumvent the rules. At the same time, how could I turn her kindness down, given the condition I was in? I smiled and thanked her profusely, and I thanked God for such a wonderful woman. It was one less thing to worry about—one less very big thing, at least for the moment.

I also received regular visits from several other people. My good friend, Danny Auguste, who worked in the city, stopped by nearly every day. My supervisor, Joaquin Gonzalez (no relation to Rosa), who had not yet arrived at work when the towers were attacked, also came by. I was elated when Joaquin told me that Joe Roque, who was the first to tell us we needed to leave the building, did just that; and he left in plenty of time to get to safety before the building fell. Joaquin also gave me some of the best news during my stay by telling me that Pasquale had somehow also survived. Having been right in front of Rosa and me when the building collapsed, he went through the same harrowing experience I did. But somehow, when all the dust settled, he found himself on top of the rubble. He was unconscious for a few hours immediately after the collapse, I was told, but eventually he woke up and was rescued, having suffered some cuts, a broken foot, and a concussion. It was wonderful to hear that the hero who led us down the steps together was rewarded with his life.

But that was where the good news ended as far as the sixteen of us who went down the stairs together were concerned.

The most emotional visit I had, a couple of days after the attacks, was from Rosa's family—specifically, her brother and the father of Rosa's daughter. They came in smiling, asking me how I was doing. But their smiles quickly turned into looks of sadness as they nervously asked me what I could tell them about the last time I saw Rosa. They had been looking for her for two days, putting posters up around town, knowing in their hearts she was likely gone, but holding out hope. Sadly, I couldn't give them any. I tried hard not to cry as I told them about our going down the stairs and losing hold of each other at the last moment. They thanked me for telling them what I could, then pulled out a picture of her that they wanted me to have. That's when I couldn't hold it in any longer and began to sob. I continued to cry every night for several nights as I looked at that photo and thought about losing her . . . and Susan . . . and all the people in our group. I even asked God if He could perform some more of His miracles and help their families find them alive. I knew that wasn't going to happen, but praying to Him about it was all I could do. It made for some very long, lonely, tearful nights.

Several members of Roger's and my families also visited. It seemed like one of them was always there, and it helped the days go by a little faster. What was so crazy, though, was that their visits were such joyous occasions for me but not so much for them. That's because they had this notion, as did some of the doctors, that the trauma I had been through would hit me hard one day all at once, causing anxiety attacks or nightmares. Some were concerned that I hadn't shown more emotion to that point and were waiting for me to come out of some kind of shock they thought I was in. They didn't know about my quiet cries at night or that the transformation I'd gone through in finding God was more than just words. There was enough concern that they requested a psychiatrist come in to talk to me.

"Really, I'm fine," I kept telling him.

He continued to press with all kinds of questions, as if he knew me better than I did. He even asked me about my childhood.

Is he kidding? I thought. I had just lived through one of the most terrifying experiences anyone could live through, and he's going to go back to my days as a happy child in Trinidad to try and figure out why I wasn't being emotional? His intentions were good. Everybody who was concerned about me had good intentions. But what they didn't know, and what they were about to find out, was that God was my psychiatrist. I talked to Him every day, several times a day. I read His book and found so many passages that pertained to my life. I was a new creation. And all I wanted to do was get home and start my new life.

CHAPTER EIGHTEEN

A New Creation

I was released from the hospital on October 29. It had been forty-eight very long days and nights since I'd left the sweet comfort of my home to go to work on September 11. Never could I have possibly imagined when I bolted out the front door, invigorated and dolled up that glorious morning, that I would return home nearly two months later battered, bruised, wearing sweats, and not caring in the least what I looked like.

Autumn had begun to show its colors. The temperature was in the upper fifties, and the trees were losing their leaves. It was difficult to fathom that it was still summer when I was last at home. But other than that, nothing had really changed. The apartment was clean. I was able to maneuver around it pretty well with my crutches and cane. While Roger took some time off work my first few days home, there was really no reason for him to be there after that. Therapists came by the house a couple of days a week for my physical therapy. His sister, Camille, routinely stopped by to help out. Roger called me all the time when he was at work to check on me. Otherwise, I couldn't do much besides read, watch television, and exercise. I occasionally had visitors over, and even our landlord was kind enough to help me if I needed anything. For the most part, though, it was a pretty quiet time. I cherished this quiet time, as it gave me a chance to reflect on my life, on how much it had changed since 9/11 and on how much it would continue to change as I grew closer to God.

While I was buried alive, I had solemnly vowed to God that I would change and become the person He wanted me to be, no matter what. My promise was more than an empty resolution. I had been transformed.

I knew that it was time to act on my promises to Him. During my physical rehab, I set three short-term goals for myself toward continuing my transformation: get baptized, get married, and find Paul—the man who first found me and deserved every bit of my gratitude.

When I told Roger about my desire to get baptized, he was completely on board. And I didn't mean I would do it in a month or a year or whenever I got around to it. I knew that one of the best and surest ways to keep a promise was to make it a priority in my life. I wasn't going to let my vows to God languish.

So on my second day home I called the Brooklyn Tabernacle and told them I wanted to be baptized. I had attended a service there over the summer with my friend Gail Fuentes, whom I watched being baptized. While I wasn't a churchgoer at the time,

I was impressed with the service. The church had thousands of congregants of all ages and races, a world-renowned choir, and a pastor who had been there for nearly thirty years. Watching Gail be baptized was a very powerful moment, as was watching all of the support she had from the congregation through prayer and music. It moved me enough that I knew that was where I wanted to be baptized.

When I called, I was told I needed to attend a couple of classes to learn more about what I was getting into and to hear some scriptures from the Bible relating to my baptism. To my surprise, not only did they have classes starting the next day, but I could have them finished in time to get baptized on the following Wednesday evening, November 7. Talk about not wasting time!

The classes were wonderful and reaffirmed that getting baptized was what I wanted to do. We each got a Bible study book, one that I still often refer to. We had some question-and-answer sessions on Scripture. We were also told about the baptism itself, including where we were supposed to be and what would take place at each step. What resonated with me more than anything was that we were told we were not out there for us, but would be representing Jesus. It was all about Him and our eternal and complete dedication to Him. That meshed with the new me and confirmed in my mind that this first goal was the right goal.

While I was taking those classes that week, I was also working on the second goal: marriage. The time Roger and I spent together in the hospital confirmed more than ever that he was the right man for me. It didn't matter to him that the attractive woman he met in Trinidad looked about as unattractive as a person could look after 9/11—dirty, distorted, bruised, broken. He ate the awful hospital food with me, watched television with me, read the Bible with me, worked with me on my rehabilitation. Not only did our love for each other strengthen, but we became best friends in the process.

When it came time to go home from the hospital, my sister, Celia, who lived in Pennsylvania, wanted me to go back with her so that she could take care of me around the clock. But Roger wanted me to remain with him in our apartment so that he could take care of me—and I wanted him to have the chance to do that. That is why it was so important to me that we get married right away—I wanted to be with him but did not want to live in sin any longer. Born and raised in the Catholic faith, I was taught that premarital sex was wrong. It was another teaching that I had ignored. Even though I hadn't been to a Catholic church for so long and was now joining a nondenominational Christian church, it still meant the world to me to follow that teaching. It was one of the vows I made to God while I was buried alive, and I was going to keep it.

None of these thoughts of marriage were a shock to Roger. We had talked about it in the past, and he had even gone as far as recently talking with his father about marrying me. It was something his dad supported and something Roger wanted as much as I did.

"Why not next week?" I said to him a day or two after I was home. No time like the present! Neither one of us was particular about what kind of wedding we had. We didn't need anything elaborate. Given my physical condition and the immediacy in wanting to do it, we were both content with the justice of the peace.

"How about next Wednesday?" I asked. "A wedding in the

morning and baptism in the evening!" The thought was over-whelmingly wonderful, and Roger was all for it.

When November 7 arrived, I couldn't have been happier. We went down to city hall in Manhattan, with Corey swinging by on his way to work to be our witness. The ceremony, including sign-ing the necessary paperwork, took maybe twenty minutes. It was one of the quickest, simplest, most uneventful ceremonies pos-sible. It also carried as much, if not more, weight to Roger and me than any elaborate, year-long-planned marriage ceremony could have. The thought that I was facing death just a few blocks away less than two months earlier and that I was now back in the city with the man I loved to begin my new life was astonishing. But the best, at least on the spiritual side, was still to come.

After going home and relaxing for a few hours, Roger and I made our way to the church for the baptism. Several family members and friends were there, including Gail, whom I had supported in the same endeavor during the summer. There were probably about ten of us who were there to be baptized. We all met with the pastor before the ceremony to go over a few things and reaffirm how much we wanted to do this. We each wore all white clothes as a symbol of purity and were brought one at a time before the congregation and to the baptismal font. It was basically a small pool that we entered by walking up some steps, then down some steps. Because of my disability, the ushers carried me up and down the steps, and I walked with some help to the center of the pool. After the pastor read from Scripture and said some words, I was dipped backward and fully immersed in the water. When I emerged soaking wet, I felt cleansed, filled with the Holy Spirit, and like a brand-new person. It was the best feeling I ever remembered having in my life. It was a new beginning for me, while at the same time a continuation of keeping my promises I'd made to the Lord on 9/11. I felt like everything I did put a smile on God's face, something I hadn't done for Him in years. In turn, that put a smile on my face.

I was now ready to continue on to my third goal: finding Paul.

CHAPTER NINETEEN

A New Light

I actually started my search for Paul while I was in the hospital. I obviously couldn't get on my feet and go out looking for him, but I told everybody I knew about what he had done and asked them to keep their eyes and ears open. Maybe his name would be mentioned on television, and I could find him that way.

I thought a lot about what Paul had done for me and how his presence unfolded. I could still feel the strength of his hand as he grabbed mine and held on to me tightly, assuring me with his words and his grip that he was not going to let me go. But there were still some things I could not figure out.

Why could I not see any light after my hand punched through the top of the rubble and he grabbed me? True, my head was turned to the side and flat on the ground because it was pinned by the concrete, so I really had to strain my head and eyes to try and see above me, but why wouldn't I have been able to see at least a stream of light? It was Wednesday morning and the sun was shining. I know all the dust made the area hazy, but not dark. I supposed it was possible that Paul was lying down on his stomach as he held my hand and part of his body or clothing blocked the light. Or maybe there was so much debris between us that there was only enough room for our hands to get through. But no light at all?

Then there was our whole confusing conversation.

"They're almost here," he said many times.

Had he been combing the area by himself when he found me? I would have thought that rescuers would have worked in teams. And how far away were they that he could see them but wasn't yelling to them that he had found me? How did they know that he found me? I hadn't heard him use a radio to contact anyone. But maybe he did and I just wasn't paying attention.

Then there was the moment when the fireman found me.

"Can you see the light?" he shouted to me.

"No, I can't see anything," I yelled back.

Then Paul said, "Hang on, Genelle. They'll get you."

Why did he keep saying "they" would get me? Wasn't he part of "they?" And why did it seem like he was communicating with me but not with the fireman? Then just before he left, after the fireman and the others found me, Paul said I was in good hands and he was going to let them do their jobs. What was *his* job? And why wouldn't he want to stay to finish what was truly his time to shine as the hero who found a survivor?

So many unanswered questions, and I knew they would remain unanswered until I found him.

Smoke and flames poured out of the top floors of the North Tower, the building I was in, before it collapsed. (Photograph by David Karp/Associated Press)

This was the second-floor window of a building at Ground Zero that Rick Cushman had to climb through to get on top of the rubble. Rick's keen eye during his search for survivors on September 12 helped lead rescuers to me. (Photograph by Rick Cushman)

Canadian police officer James Symington and his search-and-rescue dog, Trakr—whose nose sensed on September 12, 2001, that someone was alive in the area where I was buried—were photographed on the World Trade Center rubble the day after I was found. (Photograph by Stephen Chernin/Associated Press)

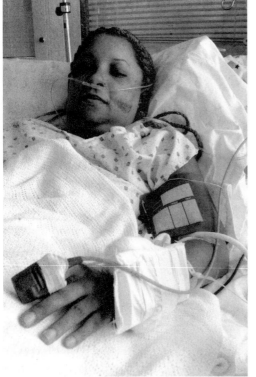

This was taken of me in Bellevue Hospital Center on September 14, 2001—three days after the attacks and two days after I was found. (Photograph by Paul Chiasson/Associated Press)

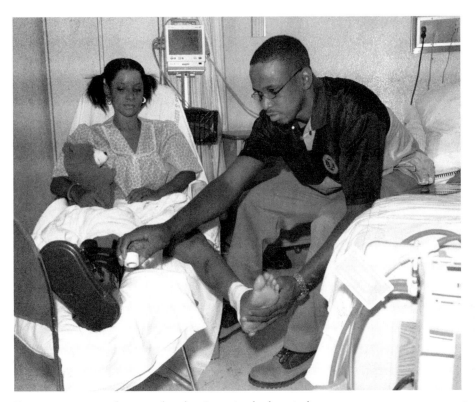

Roger was at my side every day that I was in the hospital.
(Photograph by Charlie Varley/Sipa Press)

I didn't care what I looked like after 9/11, as is evident by the T-shirt and pigtails in this photo taken of me in the hospital soon after the attacks. I was just happy to be alive. (Photograph by Chris Mitchell)

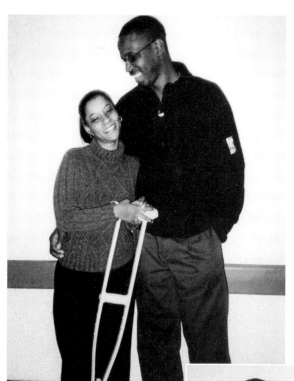

I looked and felt much better in this photo, taken just before I left the hospital after spending more than six weeks there. (Photograph by Chris Mitchell)

My stepson, Kadeem, posed with me in this photo that shows some of my scars. It was taken at our apartment in Brooklyn soon after I got home from the hospital. (Photograph by John Roca/Rex USA)

I left Kimberly behind in Trinidad in 2000, but we have been inseparable since the attacks on 9/11. This was taken in our Brooklyn apartment in the early 2000s. (Photograph by Roger McMillan)

Dominic, a stylist from Stephen Knoll Salon, worked on my hair before my wedding on CBS's *The Early Show* in the summer of 2002. (Photograph by Scott Whittle/WireImage/ Getty Images)

Me in my wedding dress before exchanging vows with Roger on CBS's *The Early Show* in the summer of 2002. (Photograph by Scott Whittle/WireImage/ Getty Images)

Roger and I were very grateful to God to be celebrating Kaydi's dedication in 2003 with the members of the Brooklyn Tabernacle. The ceremony was led by our pastor, Jim Cymbala.

My mom, Kathleen Guzman, was my hero. She posed for this photo in Pennsylvania during her visit to the United States in 1999, just months before she died of cancer. (Photograph by Carla Guzman)

Me with my sisters, Christine (center), and Mavis (right) in my Long Island, NY, neighborhood. Christine fainted after I called from the North Tower. Mavis and I were my mom's primary caregivers in Trinidad after Mom was diagnosed with cancer. (Photograph by Kaydi McMillan)

We took this picture at JFK Airport just days after our nationally-televised wedding in the summer of 2002. We were there because Roger's father, Cecil McMillan (left), was going back home to Trinidad. Next to him is Roger's brother, Corey McMillan, who was at Roger's side every moment after the attacks. On the right is their sister, Camille, who was also with Roger every step of the way. (Photograph by Marlon McMillan)

This is our family today: Roger, Kimberly, me, Kadeem, Kaydi, and Kellie. (Photograph courtesy of Digital Attractions Inc.)

While I was in the hospital, I was visited by Gary Tuchman, a journalist with CNN who had been covering the event of 9/11 since it first happened. I did some interviews with him and asked him for one favor—to help me find Paul. I told him the entire story, and he was genuinely interested in finding the man who saved my life. Through his research, Gary was able to locate Rick and Brian and reunited us on camera soon after the attacks so that I could thank them for what they had done. But Gary had no luck finding anybody named Paul. And when I asked Rick and Brian about him, they just looked at me with bewilderment.

"I really didn't know anybody's name," Rick said.

He told me how everything had unfolded from his perspective—how he spotted the fireman's jacket, then called for another fireman to come up and get him. I told him I remembered the fireman unburying me, holding my hand, and talking to me as the other rescuers freed me. But I wanted to know about the man who was holding my hand before the fireman reached me.

"There wasn't anybody else there," Rick said, seemingly perplexed by my question.

"Do you know what the fireman's name was?" I asked.

Neither had any idea.

The more I thought about Paul and tried to figure out who he was, the more confused I became. I know he was there. There was no doubt about it. I talked to him. He held my hand. I must have said his name a million times after he left so I wouldn't forget it. I know he held my hand for what seemed like an eternity, until the other rescuers arrived. I know he talked to me and updated me on what he could see. If they hadn't rescued me right after that, I might think that I was hallucinating about him, but they did save me, just as he said they would. How could nobody have seen him? I started to wonder if the fireman could have been Paul. People saw him, but nobody seemed to know his name. I guess it was possible . . . maybe. But wait—how could it have been him if Rick was the one who called him to the scene? That means the firefighter wasn't there ahead of anybody else.

Oy vey! I never thought that trying to track down a hero would be . . .

Wait a minute.

I replayed the conversations with Paul over and over and over in my mind while I was in the hospital and in the weeks after I got home. But there was part of the story I realized I hadn't considered—the very beginning. I thought long and hard about how it all started. After punching my hand through the debris and creating the hole, I tried to remove some of the debris around it. That didn't work and I was getting kind of tired, so I dozed off into a sort of half trance for a bit, all the while keeping my hand in that hole. Then I was awakened by the sirens and beeping noises. Once I realized I wasn't dreaming, I screamed:

"I'm down here! Can you see me? Please help me!"

It was right after that when I felt Paul's hand grab mine and heard those words, the ones I said were the four sweetest words I have ever heard:

"I've got you, Genelle."

Wait . . . How did he know my name? How could anyone have known my name at that time?

I will never forget those words. I will never forget him saying my name. As crazy as it sounds, I hadn't thought about that since the day he found me. I knew at the time that he said my name, but I guess after being buried alive for a day, I didn't ask myself, *So how does this person know me?* All that mattered to me at the time was that I had been found after a day of being buried alive.

I also considered the fireman and remembered that he *did* ask me my name. So the fireman couldn't have been Paul. They were two different people for sure. There *was* someone named Paul there, and he was there *before* the fireman and the others got there and would have been there while they were there—yet Rick said there was nobody there before the fireman.

This new information—actually, this old information that I finally pieced together—consumed my mind for days. Roger and I tried to figure it out, but it was like trying to put together a puzzle with a missing piece. No matter how many different ways we tried, we just couldn't solve it.

I finally decided I wasn't going to be able to figure this out on my own. I called my pastor at the Brooklyn Tabernacle, Jim Cymbala, to try and get some help in deciphering all this. I explained it all to him, from beginning to end. He listened intently, then paused for a bit to give it some deep thought.

"Who did you think Paul was?" he asked me.

"I guess I don't know," I said, unsure whether to say the word I hadn't stopped thinking.

"Genelle, let me tell you a story," he said. He proceeded to tell me the story about Paul from the Bible's book of Acts. Paul, who was originally named Saul, was a horrible person who hated Jesus and was going to Damascus to try and find His followers to bring them back to Jerusalem for persecution. The more Pastor got into it, chills went up and down my spine. There were certainly differences between Paul's story and my story, but there were too many similarities for me to ignore.

> *As he journeyed he came near Damascus, and suddenly a light shone around him from heaven. Then he fell to the ground, and heard a voice saying to him, "Saul, Saul, why are you persecuting Me?"*
>
> *And he said, "Who are You, Lord?"*
>
> *Then the Lord said, "I am Jesus, whom you are persecuting. It is hard for you to kick against the goads."*
>
> *So he, trembling and astonished, said, "Lord, what do You want me to do?"*
>
> *Then the Lord said to him, "Arise and go into the city, and you will be told what you must do."*
>
> *And the men who journeyed with him stood speechless, hearing a voice but seeing no one. Then Saul arose from the ground, and when his eyes were opened he saw no one. But they led him by the hand and brought him into Damascus. And he was three days without sight, and neither ate nor drank. (9:3–9)*

In the meantime, the Lord appeared to a man named Ananias in a vision. He told him to find Saul because Saul had seen in a vision that a man named Ananias put his hand on him and restored his sight. Ananias was skeptical because he had heard about Saul seeking out Christians to harm them, but Ananias followed the Lord's orders anyway.

> *And Ananias went his way and entered the house; and laying his hands on him he said, "Brother Saul, the Lord Jesus, who*

appeared to you on the road as you came, has sent me that
you may receive your sight and be filled with the Holy Spirit."
Immediately there fell from his eyes something like scales, and
he received his sight at once; and he arose and was baptized.

So when he had received food, he was strengthened. Then
Saul spent some days with the disciples at Damascus. Immedi-
ately he preached the Christ in the synagogues, that He is the
son of God. (9:18–19)

To say the least, I was stunned by how much my story mir-
rored Paul's.

"You were asking God for a miracle, right?"

He said that given the situation I was in and based on my story
I told him, the Paul who held my hand under the rubble may have
been that miracle.

"Genelle," Pastor said, "God may have sent you an angel."

CHAPTER TWENTY

Counting My Blessings

If I were to count my blessings each day, the counting would never end.

I couldn't have completed 2001 in a better way than by getting baptized and married and reading the Bible every day for inspiration. It was a fantastic way to close out an otherwise horrendous year and was a good springboard going into 2002—a year primarily focused on rehabilitation as I progressed from crutches, to a cane, to needing no help at all. But it was also the busiest and most significant year of my life.

The first item I had to work through was my immigration issue. While my boss at the temp agency had handled the medical matter, I assumed I was still in the country illegally and that after I was rehabilitated, I might have to go back to Trinidad. Even though I was now married and Roger was considered a resident of the country, he wasn't a U.S. citizen. How did that factor in? I honestly didn't know. And if the marriage allowed me to stay in the country, would the months prior that I was here illegally just be erased from everyone's memories? I wasn't sure, but if I had to go back to Trinidad, I would. I didn't want to, but more than anything else, I wanted to do what was right.

To my surprise, though, many people reached out to help me with my immigration status. I believe they helped for a couple of reasons. The main one was because of all the trauma I'd been through as a result of 9/11. I certainly wasn't looking for sympathy, but I'm sure that played a role. I think another reason was that I hadn't illegally immigrated. I had originally come here on a visa. And although my continued stay was illegal, I think they gave me some points for taking the initial first steps.

The person who helped me begin to resolve the issue was Virginia Fields, the borough president of Manhattan. I don't know how she knew about my situation, but she called me out of the blue one day and gave me a phone number for Senator Hillary Clinton's office, suggesting that I talk to people there about it. Really? Senator Clinton was going to help me? Roger contacted the office for me, not quite sure what to expect, but we assumed it had to be some good news. They knew who I was when Roger called. They told him to come in and pick up some paperwork to get the ball rolling on permanent residency for me. I wasn't sure what to think at first—my emotions were very mixed. I was obviously extremely excited, but I was also feeling guilty that this latest development was triggered because of something that had happened to me and not because I followed the proper procedures. But I prayed hard about it and knew God had forgiven me for it months earlier and that I could do so much good by staying in the country—not just for myself, but for Roger, who was firmly rooted in his job, and for Kimberly, who could finally come to America to live with me and experience the endless opportunities this country had to offer. After filling out the paperwork, I went into the immigration office to be interviewed and, soon after, became a legal resident. I was very grateful for the kindness from everybody who helped make it happen. Like everything else I had promised to God, I was going to make the absolute most of this chance I'd been given.

Later that spring, I was one of dozens of people fortunate to receive the Civilian Medal of Honor from the Port Authority. The award was given to me for my "courage, will, and faith" to survive. I certainly didn't think I was deserving of the honor nearly as much as someone like Pasquale, who also received it, but I was flattered to be recognized. The bigger honor for me, however, came later in the ceremony when I was told that the Port Authority would have a job waiting for me after I finished my rehabilitation. True to their word, in 2003, I returned to work in a full-time position doing basically the same work I had been doing through the temp agency before the attack. I am happy to say that I not only continue to work for the Port Authority today but have been promoted a couple of times throughout the years.

As we moved into summer, there were two big events in my life. The first was on July 13 when Roger and I got married a second time. We hadn't planned to, but when *The Early Show* on CBS and *Brides* magazine heard about my story, they wanted to throw us a wedding for the entire nation to see. I was stunned—and also excited. They took care of absolutely every detail, even flying some of our family and friends in for the ceremony. We were interviewed on television several times in the weeks leading up to the wedding and were treated to the honeymoon suite in Manhattan's Trump Tower. It was a bit over the top, but we soaked it all in.

The good news continued right after the wedding when Kimberly came to America to live with us permanently. It was something I had been discussing with Elvis in the months leading up to it, but we ultimately let Kimberly decide. Though only thirteen, she was a very mature young woman, and we both wanted our daughter to have the best opportunities possible. She decided to live with me, primarily because she was at that age where she felt she needed a female parent and role model in her life. It was very difficult for Elvis to let her go, and difficult for her to leave him, but he always wanted what was best for his daughter and understood her decision. The two of them are still extremely close, and she visits him in Trinidad at least once a year.

The last bit of big news that year, as if it couldn't get any better, was that I became pregnant. Considering that a nurse had told me the previous fall that I wouldn't be able to have children, this was indeed a major milestone. And though I was thirty-one years old with a teenage daughter already (and Roger had an eleven-year-old son, Kadeem, from a previous marriage, who was living with us), it was very exciting to know that Roger and I would be having our first child together. Kaydi was born in 2003, and we were blessed again in 2005 with the birth of Kellie.

I also spent a good part of that year becoming involved in my church, volunteering with various groups there, and eventually volunteering with the Red Cross. Considering what the church and Red Cross had done for me, I felt it was the least I could do to try and give back to them.

It was a pretty remarkable year in every respect, one that propelled me forward into the life I had promised God I would live. I've been given so much since 9/11—from this country and from countless strangers and friends alike—that I don't know any possible way I will ever be able to repay them. I wish I knew every rescuer, doctor, nurse, and anyone else who played any role in my being alive today so that I could personally thank them. The only way I know to thank them is to live a life that God would be proud of and to not keep my story to myself but to share it with others and perhaps give them some guidance and hope in their lives. So many people have inspired me since 9/11—I hope I can pay it forward and do the same for others.

CHAPTER TWENTY-ONE

9/11 Stories

In the days following 9/11, there was no escaping the tragedy for anybody. Whether you were someone like me who experienced the event firsthand, or someone living on the other side of the country with no ties to the World Trade Center outside of being an American, the news of that day took over every minute of everybody's life. There were the investigative pieces in which reporters were trying to put together who was responsible for the terrorism, how they did it, how long they had planned it, and what their mission was. There were the gut-wrenching stories of the widows and children of those who were killed who now had to continue living without their loved ones. There were the stories of the true heroes who helped save lives, in some cases sacrificing their own in the process.

For the first several days that I was in the hospital, I was in no mood to watch the television. Some of the people who visited me told me some details of the attacks, and I eventually worked up the nerve to turn on the television to see for myself. It was difficult beyond description to relive what happened. At first I didn't understand most of it. A terrorist group from the Middle East did this? They attacked the Port Authority of New York and New Jersey? On a Tuesday morning? And killed themselves in the process? On purpose? To see the physical and emotional damage from all the different perspectives that television showed was painful. But I felt like I had to watch because outside of seeing that early, brief report in the conference room while we were still in the tower, I hadn't seen anything about what happened or why it happened. I didn't even have confirmation that it wasn't an accident. And so I watched the reports, as agonizing as they were, and tried to process it all: four airplanes hijacked from three different cities at roughly the same time—one crashed into the Pentagon, another went down in a field in Pennsylvania, and two smashed into the Twin Towers.

When considering the people on the planes, in the Pentagon, and in and around the World Trade Center, more than three thousand people lost their lives. There were also hundreds who responded to the scene and died years later because of all the toxins they were exposed to during their rescue efforts.

It took a while for my brain to absorb all of this. I understood what happened, but to try and place myself in the midst of it was surreal. I know I was there. I had the physical and mental scars to prove it. But to think that I was at home that morning concerned about nothing but Roger and my Miami vacation and going to work and then somehow ending up a victim in the worst attack on American soil in the history of our country was incomprehensible.

There are few people who do not know where they were and what they were doing when they first learned of the attacks. Everybody has a story, whether he or she was a victim, relative of a victim, responder, eyewitness, or simply going about a daily routine and saw it unfold on television. But the stories I found most compelling were stories I read from Port Authority documents posted on the Internet a couple of years after 9/11 that probably very few people in the general public have ever heard or read. They are stories that were told in the months following the attacks by people who were in the heart of all the devastation as it was happening, such as police and people trapped in the buildings. Other gripping stories were transcripts, also from the Port Authority and released on the Internet, from the flood of calls that poured into the Port Authority police during the attacks. Many of the stories and transcripts are a few pages long, so I've just pulled short excerpts from some of them to give a different perspective. They feature the raw circumstances and emotions that people experienced as they tried to escape, tried to save others, or tried to do their jobs—all at such a frenzied pace and with very little knowledge of just how dire the situation was. I chose these because I was able to relate to them in some way—not just as someone who was also in the midst of all the tragedy, but in a deeper, personal way. They also helped me understand even more the hell people went through in and around other parts of the towers, and the sacrifices that were made.

Written on December 12, 2001, by a Port Authority employee in the North Tower:

I had to lead and help the elderly woman over various debris piles as we tried to exit through the turnstiles and out the West Street doors. When we arrived at the West Street doors, the elderly lady froze, screaming "Help them. I can't leave without helping them." I looked down and saw that the driveway was littered with bodies. I told the woman that there was nothing that we could do at that point and to keep moving. She was frozen solid in place. Another unknown young man who accompanied us down the stairs was pulling her arms forward while I was pushing her forward. She would not budge. Finally she moved.

Those men who helped pull and push that woman to safety remind me so much of people like Joe, Pat, Pasquale, Steve, and others on our floor who did what they could to help the rest of us. And that woman was also like them in the sense that she did not want to leave behind those people who were on the ground and couldn't help themselves. There was so much helplessness everywhere people turned, yet everybody who could grasp on to a piece of hope did it. There were so many heroes that day, and I think relatively unknown stories like this are proof that we'll never know just how many there truly were.

Written on March 5, 2002, by a Port Authority police officer:

I ran north on Church Street, trying to breathe through the thick dust, not sure how many blocks I ran, turning east onto an unknown street. A woman outside a door asked me, "Do you need water? Are you okay?" I said "I need a phone. I have to call my wife and tell her I'm okay. I know she's watching this on TV." She said "Come in and use my phone." Upon entering, I realized this was a daycare center, and I saw about fourteen or fifteen children. I told her she had to leave immediately. "TAKE THE CHILDREN, LEAVE RIGHT NOW, AND KEEP GOING NORTH TOWARD THE GWB (George Washington Bridge)," to which she immediately complied. I tried to call home and found the telephone lines were inoperable.

I look at Kaydi and Kellie and am reminded of 9/11 every single day. They are so precious to Roger and me, because we both know our girls would not be here if I had died. And when they are not with us, such as when they are at school, we are putting their lives in the hands of other people and expect that anybody there would do whatever necessary to protect them and the other children from harm. To read what that officer did reaffirmed for me the basic goodness in people. Who knows how many people he helped to safety before feeling the need to escape for his own life. But then what does he do when he stops to call his wife and tell her he's okay? He starts thinking about others again when he sees the faces of those children. And the teacher, without hesitation, followed his orders. Those are the kind of people you want with your kids when you cannot be.

Written on March 8, 2002, by a Port Authority police officer:

> *I recall watching the towers burning and hearing Sgt. Kohl-mann screaming as the building fell; however, I have no visual recollection of the collapse (I must have been looking at it, but somehow the image is gone from my mind).*

I found this passage fascinating because after 9/11, when Pasquale and I did various, separate interviews about our experiences, I noticed that he was quoted as saying we were on the twenty-second floor when the tower collapsed, while I have always said we were on the thirteenth floor. I was stunned at his claim. He was stunned at my claim. How could two people, both of us seemingly with our wits about us and one walking right behind the other down the stairs, remember something like that as being so different? To this day, I'm sure we still probably don't agree on where exactly we were. It doesn't matter, but it just fascinates me how the human mind works in certain situations.

Written on November 1, 2001, by a Port Authority police officer:

> *I began to run north, down West Street; people were running all over in each direction. Two women tripped on one of the*

high curbs and were on the ground; they were being tripped over and run over by others fleeing the collapse.

I can only pray that someone eventually stopped to help those women or that they were able to get up on their own. Reading this really magnified for me the terror going on in other areas of the complex because it was not at all the perspective I had. How long were we in the tower after the plane hit? It was about seventy-five minutes before we even decided to leave. There was initially very little panic on our floor and never any mad rush like there was outside.

Written on November 28, 2001, by a Port Authority police officer:

When we entered the city, the first thing you noticed was the foot of ash on the ground. Various fire equipment scattered from block to block, cut firemen leaning up against the store-fronts as their colleagues try to help them.

I can imagine this as a painting—a row of firefighters with their equipment off, expressions of agony, cuts and bruises, sweat dripping from their bodies, wanting so desperately to get back to the towers and help people, because it's what they do for a living and what they are all about as human beings. It reminded me of the fireman spotted by Rick underneath me. Even in death, his presence helped save my life.

Transcript of a phone conversation between a man named Greg at NBC News and a Port Authority police sergeant:

OFFICER: *"Sergeant Murriano."*

GREG: *"Sergeant, it's Greg at NBC News. I need to put anybody on the air by telephone, to try and tell us what's happening. Can you help me?"*

OFFICER: *"How can we know? I'm looking [at] what you're looking at on the TV."*

GREG: *"Can you tell me what you know?"*

OFFICER: *"I don't know anything yet."*

GREG: *"Can you tell me what you're looking at?"*

OFFICER: *"You don't . . . you don't have a television?"*

GREG: *"I do . . ."*

OFFICER: *"It looks like a big hole in the top of One World Trade."*

GREG: *"Is there anybody that can go on the telephone?"*

OFFICER: *"It's too early for that."*

GREG: *"How soon can I try to do that? Tell me what's . . . advise me how . . ."*

OFFICER: *"Well, call our public affairs people . . ."*

We all face stress at work, but this was a great example to me of two people trying to do their jobs, and doing them in a polite way with each other, in one of the most stressful work environments ever. The officer is being kind but bluntly honest with the reporter. He can't be giving it to him any straighter than he is. The reporter is also being kind but trying to squeeze whatever information he can out of the officer to inform the world of what is happening in the most detailed way that he can. Aside from the rescuers, one has to appreciate the work that so many people like this did that day, especially considering the spontaneity of the situation and the enormous devastation that resulted.

Transcript of a phone conversation between a gentleman at the George Washington Bridge and a Port Authority police officer:

OFFICER: *"Port Authority Police, Officer Maggett."*
MAN: *"Hey, Maggett, this is Faracia from the GWB."*
OFFICER: *"What's your name again, I'm sorry."*
MAN: *"Faracia, from the George Washington Bridge."*
OFFICER: *"Uh-huh."*
MAN: *"Angelo, how are you doing?"*
OFFICER: *"All right, brother."*
MAN: *"What happened down there?"*
OFFICER: *"Well, we're not sure whether a plane crashed into the building, or an explosion."*
MAN: *"Is anybody hurt down there."*
OFFICER: *"A lot of people are just . . . it's unconfirmed, but there might be one or . . . a couple of DOAs."*
MAN: *"Oh my God! What building?"*
OFFICER: *"Building one."*
MAN: *"All right, thanks."*

One or a couple of people dead—maybe. No matter how many times I read that, it's still amazing to think that was the initial impression, but it shows how little people knew right away.

It was exactly the way I and others were thinking at the time. Was it an explosion? A plane? A little plane? It's why people like me hung around.

The following transcripts are of three phone conversations between a woman named Christine who worked at Windows on the World (a 106th- and 107th-floor restaurant area in the North Tower) and a Port Authority police officer:

OFFICER: *"Port Authority Police, Murray."*

CHRISTINE: *"Hi, this is Christine up at Windows on 107. We are still waiting for direction. We have guests up here."*

OFFICER: *"Ah, how many people have you got there, up there, approximately?"*

CHRISTINE: *"We have approximately probably about seventy-five to a hundred people."*

OFFICER: *"Seventy-five to a hundred, and you're up on 106 or 107?"*

CHRISTINE: *"One-oh-six. One-oh-seven's impossible. The smoke condition on 107 is . . ."*

OFFICER: *"We're . . . we are sending officers and fire personnel up there at this time. We are evacuating as soon as possible."*

CHRISTINE: *"But we . . . right now we need to find a safe haven on 106 where the smoke condition isn't bad. Can you direct us to a certain quadrant?"*

OFFICER: *"All right, we are sending somebody up there as soon as possible. If anybody can get to the staircase, that's fine. We are sending up there . . ."*

CHRISTINE: *"You can't. The staircase is . . ."*

OFFICER: *"All right, we're sending . . . we're sending people up there as soon as possible."*

CHRISTINE: *"What's your ETA?"*

OFFICER: *"I . . . ma'am, I have to get on the radio. As soon as possible. As soon as it's humanly possible."*

CHRISTINE: Hangs up.

About five minutes later:

OFFICER: *"Port Authority Police, Murray."*

CHRISTINE: *"Hi, this is Christine again from Windows on the World."*

OFFICER: *"Okay, uh, ma'am, as soon as is possible. I've notified everybody to be notified to get up there."*

CHRISTINE: Hangs up.

About four minutes later:

OFFICER: *"Port Authority Police, Murray."*

CHRISTINE: *"Hi, this is Christine again, from Windows on the World on the 106th floor. The situation on 106 is rapidly getting worse."*

OFFICER (TO PEOPLE IN THE BACKGROUND): *"I got a fourth call from Windows on the World. It's getting rapidly worse up there."*

CHRISTINE: *"We . . . we have . . . the fresh air is going down fast! I'm not exaggerating."*

OFFICER: *"Uh, ma'am, I know you're not exaggerating.*

We're getting a lot of these calls. We are sending the fire
department up as soon as possible. I have you, Christine,
four calls, seventy-five to a hundred people, Windows on
the World, 106th floor."
CHRISTINE: *"What are we going to do for air?"*
OFFICER: *"Ma'am, the fire department . . ."*
CHRISTINE: *"Can we break a window?"*
OFFICER: *"You can do whatever you have to to get to, uh,*
the air."
CHRISTINE: *"All right."*

That was the last call I could find from Christine. I feel those
phone calls she made epitomize the sadness, desperation, and
hopelessness that so many people felt that day. There's Christine,
the leader and potential hero to as many as a hundred people,
trying to get help and find solutions to escape the terror that was
strangling them with each passing minute. And there's the police
officer, who is constantly answering phone calls from frantic people and trying to find the solutions they're yearning for in a situation that is far beyond anybody's control, including his. Those calls
are a painful reminder of what thousands of people experienced
that day, and that many continue to live through today because
of injuries they suffered, or because of the void left in their lives
by the loss of their loved ones. It's all the more reason why I need
to continue asking "Why me?" and never stop asking until I find
the answers.

CHAPTER TWENTY-TWO

Why Me?

During my hospital stay, and in the first few months after I got out, what people saw in me more than anything else were the physical challenges I faced. But the toughest challenge I dealt with was the question that the psychiatrist never posed, one that was mentally bogging me down more and more with each passing day:

Why me?

It started to creep into my mind after Rosa's family visited me in the hospital, grew stronger as I learned about all the people who lost their lives, and overwhelmed me soon after I was discharged from the hospital and received an unexpected phone call from Susan's mother.

Susan was very close to her mom, even living with her to take care of her. When her mom called and told me who she was, I was so stunned that I almost dropped the phone. She said she struggled to get up the courage to call, and it was just as uncomfortable for me because that's when the survivor's guilt really set in. I was alive and her daughter wasn't. Why? How was that fair? I bet if you put our life resumes side by side, her's trumped mine easily. Why was I here and she wasn't? I didn't have a clue, and that bothered me.

I had no idea what to say to her mom at first and was actually whispering a little prayer in my heart as she was talking, asking God to bless me with the right words for this mother who was still mourning. He did, and we were able to carry on a very nice and meaningful conversation. What she wanted, more than anything else, was to know about her daughter's last moments. I described them to her in the most positive light that I could and told her how strong her daughter was through it all, including the words of encouragement and big hug she gave me when I broke down just before we headed down the stairs. I could feel her mother's sense of relief as I told her, and I know it gave her some closure that she'd been longing for. But after we hung up, I sat alone in silence, thinking long and hard about that question: *Why me?*

I've grown to believe that everything happens for a reason. There is a reason why we headed down the stairs when we did, and not sooner. There is a reason why the building collapsed when it did, and not a second sooner or later. There is a reason why I was buried alive under the rubble. There is a reason why some people escaped unharmed. There is a reason why some died. And I believe God is behind every one of those reasons. What is difficult for us to accept as human beings, and was difficult for me to accept after my rescue, is that we don't always know the reason for something happening at the time it happens. Sometimes it takes days, weeks, months, years, or even an entire lifetime before we get the answers we hope for. Sometimes we die without knowing, but perhaps we find out in the next life. In my case today, I'm still searching for the answer.

I think about the question every single day and am sure I always will. The quietest moment of my day is when I drive to work every morning, and I often use that time to listen for answers. I play gospel music, talk to God as if He's riding in the passenger seat, and watch the people and things around me for signs.

Sometimes I'll get a call on my phone from a church pastor asking me to come and speak about my experience. Being able to share my story is a part of the answer to "Why me?" Being a survivor from that day changed me, and telling my story to others has helped them become better stewards of their lives, better parents, better friends, better children. I know that because people tell me so after I speak. But God could have picked any one of the innocent people who perished to do this work.

I've also wondered if maybe there is something I'm supposed to do with a family member of someone who died, something that will make the world better. Maybe it has something to do with my children. Roger and I have had two beautiful girls together since 9/11, Kaydi and Kellie. If I hadn't survived, they wouldn't exist . . . and maybe there is something they will do in twenty or thirty years that will change the world. I don't know. I wish I did. But all I can do is believe . . . and never stop searching.

I believe that asking the question, and searching for answers to it, is a responsibility I will have for life. I am responsible to ask it on behalf of those who died—Rosa, Susan, Pat, the Russian man, Steve, everybody in the World Trade Center buildings, and those in Washington, DC and Pennsylvania. I am responsible to ask on behalf of those whose loved ones died and those whose hopes died on that day. There are countless victims from 9/11. I was one of them. But I was also a survivor. And I don't know why.

I know the question—and the answer—is not about me. That's the only part of "Why me?" that I understand. There is a bigger picture. A plan. I'm a part of it, a small part, but the plan is not about me. Somehow, it is about God.

A coworker used to often ask me: "Why did God save you and not others? Why did God allow so many innocent people to be killed?" I always gave him the same answer: "I have no idea." Being a survivor doesn't make me an expert on how God thinks. Life is unpredictable and unexplainable because none of us knows what His plan is. All that I can do is trust in Him completely and in the fact that there is a huge reason why I am still alive today. I need to continue living the life that I know He wants me to live, with my eyes and ears open, believing that one day I'll understand.

CHAPTER TWENTY-THREE

Lessons Learned

We can learn something with every experience, from childhood through adulthood, and what I learn today may not necessarily be something new to me. There have been some things that I learned as a child, then forgot about or never put into practice, but learned again through an experience in my adult years. For example, I was taught how to pray as a child, never paid much attention to it, then learned how to pray again when I turned thirty. As long as we keep our minds open to every situation, there is always knowledge to be gained.

The lessons I learned while I was buried alive, and in the months following, were infinite. They were physical, mental, and spiritual. I learned so much about myself—what I am capable and incapable of doing. I learned about other people, too, from the evil of the terrorists to the heroism of countless strangers I'll never know. And I learned about God and the power He has in our daily lives.

Many of the lessons I present here may sound familiar. They may seem, in many ways, like common sense. I know they felt that way when I wrote them down. I'd heard and/or been taught most of them before. But I also realized that it had been years since I took time to meditate on them. But once I became more conscious of these lessons and took them to heart, my life and spirit have been exponentially enriched.

Never give up hope

Whether you're a Christian or a non-Christian, no matter what you believe or do not believe about a higher power, you have likely heard the parable of the prodigal son, one of the most famous stories about hope. It's not very long, but if you have never heard it or read it in its entirety, it is as follows:

A certain man had two sons. And the younger of them said to his father "Father, give me the portion of goods that falls to me." So he divided to them his livelihood. And not many days after, the younger son gathered all together, journeyed to a far country, and there wasted his possessions with prodigal living. But when he had spent all, there arose a severe famine in that land, and he began to be in want. Then he went and joined himself to a citizen of that country, and he sent him into his fields to feed swine. And he would gladly have filled his stomach with the pods that the swine ate, and no one gave him anything.

But when he came to himself, he said, "How many of my father's hired servants have bread enough and to spare, and I perish with hunger! I will arise and go to my father, and will say to him, 'Father, I have sinned against heaven and before you, and I am no longer worthy to be called your son. Make me like one of your hired servants.'" And he arose and came to his father. But when he was still a great way off, his father saw him and had compassion, and ran and fell on his neck and kissed him. And the son said to him, "Father, I have sinned against heaven and in your sight, and I am no longer worthy to be called your son."

But the father said to his servants, "Bring him out the best robe and put it on him, and put a ring on his hand and sandals on his feet. And bring the fatted calf here and kill it, and let us eat and be merry."

Now his older son was in the field. And as he came and drew near to the house, he heard music and dancing. So he called one of the servants and asked what these things meant. And he said to him, "Your brother has come, and because he has received him safe and sound, your father has killed the fatted calf."

But he was angry and would not go in. Therefore his father came out and pleaded with him. So he answered and said to his father, "Lo, these many years I have been serving you; I never transgressed your commandment at any time; and yet you never gave me a young goat, that I might make merry with my friends. But as soon as this son of yours came, who

*has devoured your livelihood with harlots, you killed the fatted
calf for him."*

*And he said to him, "Son, you are always with me, and all
that I have is yours. It was right that we should make merry
and be glad, for your brother was dead and is alive again, and
was lost and is found."* (Luke 15:11–32)

The prodigal son could have easily given up all hope that his
father would ever allow him to return home. And how easy, and
justified, it would have been for the father to give up all hope in
his son. But the son won half the battle before even coming home
by admitting his wrongdoings *to himself.* He then humbly sought
forgiveness from his father, hoping that he could begin anew.

I see my life reflecting the prodigal son's. He didn't give a
thought to how he was living when he took his inheritance and
squandered it. I was the same. But the prodigal son and I grew
embarrassed and ashamed of ourselves and knew we were not
worthy of another opportunity—but we never gave up hope, em-
barking on long, emotional journeys to become the good people
we once were.

Hope is something we all crave. We hope that our job goes well
at work, that our children are safe at school, that our house is still
standing when we return home. We hope that our car doesn't break
down, that the weather is nice, that an ill loved one gets better, that
we pass that test at school. We constantly hope, oftentimes without
even thinking about it. It's a natural part of being human.

But how do we react toward hope when facing adversity, when
that hope appears nonexistent yet is what will make the difference
between winning or losing, succeeding or not succeeding, living or

dying? When the deck is stacked against us and we're holding an almost certain losing hand, do we fold, or hold out hope for that one card that can turn everything around?

Consider the difference between the early hours and the final hours that I was buried under the rubble. When it all started, I was enclosed in total darkness, legs crushed, arm pinned, head immobile, and nobody could hear me. Toward the end, I was enclosed in total darkness, legs crushed, arm pinned, head immobile, and nobody could hear me. My physical state hadn't changed the slightest bit for the better. In fact, it worsened as I got weaker from a lack of food and water. The only difference between the beginning and the end was that, in the end, I had found hope—hope that the Lord would hear me, trust me, forgive me, and rescue me. And this was all before Paul took my hand.

I found an anonymous quote that says: *"When the world says 'Give up,' hope whispers 'Try it one more time.'"*

Hope does not discriminate. It does not matter how dire a situation may seem, how much pain or angst you are feeling, or how badly you are beaten down. It doesn't matter who you are, where you are, or in what direction you may be heading. Hope is always there. Like the prodigal son did, you must seize it. Once you do, God will be there to welcome you into His arms. Listen for hope's whisper.

Always take advantage of a second chance

It's a wonderful feeling to be given a second chance. If you get a bad grade on a test in school, sometimes a teacher will allow you to correct your mistakes for partial credit, or even retake the test. If you're at work and do something to a client's dissatisfaction, that client may come back and give you another chance to keep his business. If you're playing in a game and do something to hurt your team, there could still be enough time on the clock for you to redeem yourself. But those second-chance moments are rare, which is what makes them so precious.

Most of the time, life does not give us do-overs. The things we say, the things we do—they can never be undone. We can try to make amends. We can seek forgiveness. We can do things differently the next time. But it's those big mistakes, the ones of extreme proportions that negatively affect our lives or the lives of others, that are difficult to overcome and erase, no matter how hard we try. That is why when a second chance presents itself, it is important to recognize it, understand how fortunate we are to receive it, and take every advantage of it.

That concept never crossed my mind until 9/11. I took everything in life for granted every day—that I would wake up in the morning, that the train would get me safely to work, that the building I worked in would weather any turmoil, that I would see my friends and loved ones as planned. I didn't see life as a gift. I didn't see it as something that would one day be taken from me, even though we all know we are mortal. Like many people, especially younger generations, I felt like I was invincible, in control of my destiny at every moment. I lived life how I wanted, confident that I could go back anytime and change anything, or do something over, if necessary.

When I left Kimberly behind, it was temporary to me. Yes, I'd miss out on a year or two of her life while living away from her, but my mind-set was that I would get a chance to make up for that when I was able to bring her to New York. It was a sacrifice, but not a permanent one. My thinking was the same way when it came to my relationship with God. I wasn't very close to Him like I was raised to be as a child, but I never worried about it. I figured I'd party for a while, have some fun, do what I wanted, then maybe come back to Him later in life. But, as I found out on 9/11, life doesn't always go according to our plans. Thousands of good people that day who were expecting another routine day never got a second chance. They did not get another opportunity to say good-bye to their loved ones, to do the work they were doing, to finish that cup of coffee. Very few of us, for whatever reason, were given another chance at life that day. I felt not only fortunate, but responsible to make the most of that precious gift of life and not waste it.

One of the most famous stories of second chances, which has been told in several different forms, including children's books and cartoons, is that of Jonah and the great fish.

As the story goes, God told Jonah to go to the city of Nineveh and "cry out against it; for their wickedness has come up before Me." But Jonah decided to do his own thing instead, and he fled to the city of Tarshish to get away from God. He hopped on a ship with some other men and sailed out to sea, thinking he had escaped God's sight. But God created huge winds that were about to bust the boat into pieces. The men got nervous and, realizing it was Jonah's actions that caused God to create the turbulence, tossed him overboard. With that, the sea instantly became calm.

Meanwhile, God had a huge fish swallow Jonah, to give him

another chance. After Jonah spent three days and nights praying in the fish's belly, God heard Jonah and had the fish throw him up onto land. God then repeated his previous orders to Jonah: "Arise, go to Nineveh, that great city, and preach to it the message that I tell you." This time, Jonah did just that. He told the people that their city was about to be destroyed by God because of their wicked behavior. So they immediately changed their ways, and God spared the city His wrath.

I think that story has become so well known to people of all walks of life because of the infrequency with which second chances occur. Whether or not you believe in God, or in the Bible from which that story came, does not preclude anyone from understanding and relating to the lesson in it about second chances. Not only did Jonah get one, but so did the people of Nineveh. Second chances are rare, special moments that cannot be wasted. Third chances are almost unheard of.

I often think about how close I came to never seeing Kimberly again, how close I came to never seeing Roger again, and how close I came to never having the chance to make amends with God. I don't think of those things because they are haunting memories—I purposely think of them because I don't ever want to forget them. As depressing as it might seem for me to relive those nightmares, keeping them in the forefront of my mind at all times reminds me never to expect that tomorrow will be there. They remind me never to take anyone or anything for granted, and to realize that when I'm given another opportunity to do something, especially something I previously did wrong, no matter how big or small, I need to appreciate it and take full advantage of it.

Be prepared for death

How do we prepare for something when we have no idea when or how it will happen? How was I supposed to be prepared to die in the collapse of a 110-story tower? How was I supposed to prepare for the instantaneous deaths of my friends and coworkers? How was I supposed to be ready to die at the age of thirty?

We cannot live our daily lives in fear. Bad things are going to happen to us. They happen to everybody. That's part of life. If we live in fear, we don't live at all. But I learned from 9/11 that while I could have never been completely prepared for the tragedy that struck, I would have been more ready if I had simply lived a better life to that point.

Looking at statistics of how many people die each day shows just how precious life is. We see death constantly on the news, on the Internet, in the newspaper, when we pass funeral processions on the road—but it usually takes a personal tragedy in our lives to make us realize that it can happen to us at any moment. In the United States, in 2007, more than 2.4 million people died. That's an average of nearly 6,600 people every day. Among those deaths, more than a million were from heart disease, cancer, or stroke. But the category that really caught my eye was unintentional, or accidental, injuries. There were more than 123,000 people in 2007 who fell into that group, an average of roughly 339 accidental deaths every day. What a staggering statistic! That could be the equivalent of a schoolful of children, or an entire neighborhood of families being wiped out on a daily basis. If it happened that way, it would be categorized publicly as a tragedy, and everybody would pay more attention. But it doesn't, and they don't.

So how do we prepare our hearts for the other side of this life, which is approaching closer and closer with every passing second? It's all about leading a good life every moment of every day.

We're not going to be perfect, of course. We're not made that way. But there is so much we can do to better ourselves and, ultimately, the world around us. It can be as simple as a smile, a hello, a handshake, a hug. It can be a phone call to a loved one, or a phone call to make amends with someone we haven't been getting along with. It can be lending a helping hand, or a monetary donation, to someone who needs assistance. It can be eliminating the gossiping, the backstabbing, and the negativity at school or work. It can be a visit to someone who needs it, or a handout to a stranger who could use a boost. It can be as simple as sharing a laugh, or as difficult as sharing a cry in someone's sorrow. It can be giving advice, or just lending an ear to someone who needs one. It can be dishing out a small compliment, or throwing a huge celebration.

When I was buried alive, I realized how many of those things I had not done on a regular basis. My life was more about me than about anyone else, and that attitude nearly destroyed a lot of lives, including my daughter's and that of the man I loved. Had death taken me with the thousands of others it took that day, I'm not sure where I would be now—and it scares me to think about it.

We cannot live in fear . . . but maybe a little bit of fear is a good thing. I once saw a bumper sticker that said IF YOU DON'T BE-LIEVE IN GOD, YOU BETTER HOPE YOU'RE RIGHT. I guess you could say that's how I live my life. I cannot say for certain God exists any more than a nonbeliever can say for certain that He does not exist.

But having that little bit of fear of the unknown has helped me grow closer to Him since 9/11 and has helped me to be a better person. Whatever it takes—be it fear of God or fear of something else—lead a good life, one that makes a positive difference in the world. In the end, whenever that may be, it will leave you better prepared for the inevitable.

Enjoy the little things in life

There was a popular movie in 1986 called *Ferris Bueller's Day Off* in which Ferris, a high school teenager, skipped school with two of his friends and did about everything there was to do in Chicago, from eating at an upscale restaurant to taking in the art museum to catching a foul ball at a Cubs game. I think the theme of the comedy was imbedded in this quote from Ferris: "Life moves pretty fast. If you don't stop and look around once in a while, you could miss it."

I believe everybody should dream big. I always did. From my days as a perennial talent-contest winner when I was a teen to actually moving to New York City to try and make it big—I wanted it all. But in the process, I got swept up in the whirlwind of life and never appreciated the "little things." Rarely did I stop to take a look around.

My greatest gift in the world was Kimberly. It's heartbreaking to think about all the small, daily joys with her that I missed by living away from her. I also think about the two weeks that I was separated from Roger just before 9/11. He seemed to understand the small joys in life, like sitting at home on the couch with me and doing absolutely nothing together for an evening rather than hitting the party scene night after night.

I thought one day about how much the "little things" played a part in my life from the time I woke up on September 11 until I was rescued. There were so many of them.

It began with that good night's sleep I got, something I didn't often get because of my many late nights out. There was the cool, gentle breeze streaming through my window, the beautiful clothes I was fortunate to have, and the gorgeous sunny day that was waiting for me as I left the apartment to catch the train.

There was the quiet, peaceful, uneventful ride into town, and the nice walk from the station to my office building in the finest city in the world. There was that delicious bagel and hot chocolate that I bought, the work I had to do that reminded me how much I loved my job, and the good conversation with Susan.

While some may expect me to stop there because of what happened next, I can easily keep going. There was my friendship with Rosa that had grown in the short time we'd known each other, so strong that we stuck together like sisters throughout the entire ordeal on 9/11. There was Pasquale and others on the floor who showed enough care and concern for all of us that they nearly led us out of the building in time. There were the firefighters in the stairwell, heading up the stairs and into danger, all for our sake. And who can forget Rosa's sense of humor in the stairwell regarding my shoes?

While I was trapped, I still had my breath, my consciousness, a functioning brain. My left arm was free. My hand and fingers attached to that arm could move. It was a serene place I was in, just the kind of place to pause and say a prayer. I reflected on my childhood like never before. I relearned the prayers from my Catholic school days. I thought about the prayer Mom taught me. I thought about Mom.

I found God again. Turned out He'd never left—I had been the one hiding. I discovered a confidence in myself that I hadn't had in years, one that gave me the ability to speak to Him, and to not be afraid to ask Him for some assistance. Thinking about Kimberly made me smile. Roger, too. What blessings they were in my life.

And there was Paul. Okay, maybe Paul cannot be classified as a "little thing," but how about what he did for me? He didn't raise me above the ashes with his spiritual power. He just held my hand. He talked to me. He kept me calm. He assured me help was coming. He wasn't in a hurry. He was just there . . . for as long as he had to be.

There were Rick and Brian, who stopped to look around in their fast-paced lives and, as a result, ended up in New York. Rick just happened to glance in my direction and spot the deceased fireman. A quick glance—that's all it took, followed by a fireman stumbling upon me as he came to his brother's side. And none of them would have been searching that area without Trakr's nose. How's that for a little thing—a dog's nose. He was probably rewarded with a hearty meal after his act of courage—and that probably made him as content as could be. I found out that Trakr passed away in 2009. I never met him but will never forget him. If you believe dogs go to heaven, you know he's there, looking out for everybody.

There were the cheers as I was carried from the rubble to the waiting ambulance. The smile on my face. The smiles on the faces of the rescuers. My meeting with Roger, and the tears we shared. His comment of "Why didn't you get out when I told you to?"

That will forever be ingrained in my mind, and will always make me smile.

The day on which my life nearly ended was full of dozens of those little things, and I didn't realize a single one of them at the time. Life will move fast, but it doesn't mean you always have to keep pace. Heed Ferris's advice and take a look around once in a while. Life is a beautiful thing. You don't want to miss it.

Be happy with what you have

Alexandre Dumas, a nineteenth-century French writer, probably has the best quote that defines my attitude toward happiness:

> There is neither happiness nor misery in the world; there is only the comparison of one state to another, nothing more. He who has felt the deepest grief is best able to experience supreme happiness. We must have felt what it is to die, that we may appreciate the enjoyments of life.

I certainly died emotionally when I realized I was about to lose everything I loved. My grief could not have been any deeper as I thought about forever losing my daughter, my boyfriend, myself. It's because of the near losses of those relationships, and that love, that I do have a greater appreciation for what is important in life. I realize that happiness is not about how much money I have, how many bars I can hit in one night, how good I look, how much power I have. Many people believe the more money we have, the more freedom that will come with it. We'll be free to buy what we want, work when we want, do whatever we want whenever we want. But how true is that? Consider these words from Mother Teresa:

> The more you have, the more you are occupied, the less you give. But the less you have the more free you are. Poverty for us is a freedom. It is not mortification, a penance. It is joyful freedom. There is no television here, no this, no that. But we are perfectly happy.

Think about that. "The more you have, the more you are occupied, the less you give." How often are we prisoners to "stuff"? Our cars, our homes, our clothes. With a television, our lives and relationships often revolve around a certain movie, the big game, or a particular reality television show. Does anyone see the irony of sitting in front of a television, watching people we do not know live their lives?

I see nothing wrong with accumulating wealth or spending money on "stuff" and having some fun with it. But it's when that money or the things we buy begin to define who we are that I question whether or not we are truly happy. Norman MacEwan, a commander in the British Royal Air Force, was once quoted as saying:

> Happiness is not so much in having as sharing. We make a living by what we get, but we make a life by what we give.

The fact is that we are, in so many respects, a society of greed. We might like what we have, but we want more all the time.

Whatever the latest gadget is, we have to have it—the newest software program, latest version of a video game, hottest Christmas gift for the season, most current cell phone available. How many of us are going to be texting or tweeting from our death beds? The way technology has, in a sense, replaced true relationships, I wouldn't be surprised if it's the only communication some lonely, unhappy people will know how to use.

Aleksandr Solzhenitsyn, a Russian novelist who passed away in 2008, once said:

> One should never direct people towards happiness, because happiness too is an idol of the market-place. One should direct them toward mutual affection. A beast gnawing at its prey can be happy too, but only human beings can feel affection for each other, and this is the highest achievement they can aspire to.

Happiness is about those relationships, be it with family, friends, or God. Friends without money or material possessions can make us happy. Money or material possessions without friends? In my opinion, not so much.

I'll end this lesson I learned with one of my favorite quotes. It's a real eye-opening statement from someone who purportedly had it all—Abd-ar-Rahman III, a powerful prince in the tenth century. But he realized after five decades, after doing some math and a little soul searching, that he had very little:

> I have now reigned about 50 years in victory or peace, beloved by my subjects, dreaded by my enemies, and respected

by my allies. Riches and honors, power and pleasure, have waited on my call, nor does any earthly blessing appear to have been wanting to my felicity. In this situation, I have diligently numbered the days of pure and genuine happiness which have fallen to my lot. They amount to . . . 14.

Focus on raising your children with high morals, then trust they will follow your teachings

There is no manual that comes with the birth of a child, which I think is a sign of God's sense of humor. Instructions come with everything else. Anytime you purchase a product with "some assembly required," there is always a set of directions with it, sometimes as thick as a novel. But as those of you who are parents know, when this tiny infant comes into your life, screaming from the top of her little lungs, different from every other living person on the planet, and with the potential to be influenced every day by anything and anyone around her, you're somehow supposed to mold her into an honest, productive, contributing member of society without any formal instructions on how to do it. Is there anything more challenging in this world than raising children?

There's the physical toll of carrying them around, changing their diapers, cleaning up after them, driving them to school, helping them with homework, playing with them, coaching their sports teams. The list goes on and on, and the years dwindle from your own life with every ache, every pain, every hour of potential sleep missed.

The financial toll is felt for a lifetime: food, diapers, clothes, toys, education, health care, a car, and the incidental "Dad, can I borrow twenty bucks?" requests. I found some figures from the U.S. Department of Agriculture that show the cost of raising a child from birth to eighteen years old can range from almost $200,000 to nearly $400,000, depending on your income and the lifestyle you lead. I would guess the cost is closer to the latter figure for many, and then if you help pay for college, it skyrockets exponentially.

The mental and emotional toll cannot be quantified but is probably the most significant. As parents, we stress about the well-being of our children—the illnesses, struggles in school, and social issues that come with their growing up. The teen years bring a new set of worries with new friends, and with tougher decisions left to young, impressionable minds. The physical and financial tolls add to the mental worries. And it doesn't get any easier as they get older and move out of the house—just different. They will always be our babies. The concern will never cease.

With all of those challenges, however, I don't believe there is anything more gratifying than raising a child. To be able to take this little person at birth, whose entire existence depends on you, and mold her into a person in your image is so unbelievably spectacular that I cannot think of any gift God can give us here on earth that comes close to comparing to that experience. But with that molding comes an incredible amount of responsibility, a responsibility that can have a chain reaction and affect generations to come.

If you are a good person with high morals, the chances are pretty good your children will grow up to be the same way, because that is how you raised them to be, and because you surrounded them with positive influences and role models. If you dislike a certain group of people, odds are that your child will also grow up with that hatred, because that is what she has learned from you. If you are a Republican or a Democrat, there's a strong possibility that your child will grow up with the same party affiliation because that's what she has grown up listening to you talk about. If you are a fan of a certain sports team, your child will also likely be a fan of that team.

But one thing I've come to realize as a parent is that no matter how hard you try to raise your children to be a certain way or believe in a certain cause, they will eventually grow up and think on their own. They will make their own decisions based on what they think is right and on what they think will be best for them. That "letting go" may be the most difficult mental aspect that comes with parenting, but it also means you've done your job well.

As I read through the Bible after 9/11, I did not realize how many verses there are about children and raising them. The following are a few that caught my attention.

From Deuteronomy 6:5–7:

You shall love the LORD your God with all your heart, with all your soul, and with all your strength.

And these words which I command you today shall be in your heart. You shall teach them diligently to your children, and shall talk of them when you sit in your house, when you walk by the way, when you lie down, and when you rise up.

Another short, but compelling one, is from Ephesians 6:4:

Fathers, do not provoke your children to wrath, but bring them up in the training and admonition of the Lord.

We don't let go of our children just once, but several times throughout their lives. We let go when they start to feed themselves and no longer need a mother's milk for nutrition. We let go a little bit more when they go from elementary school to middle school, from middle school to high school, and from high school to college. We let go some more when they move away from home, get a job, and get married. The "letting go" process can be painful and rewarding at the same time. It's painful because they no longer need us like they once did for that particular task or segment of their lives. They solely depended upon us at one time but no longer do. It is also a rewarding process, though, because if we have raised our children in the light of those verses I just shared, then we've done our jobs.

That leads me to one more verse, from Proverbs 22:6:

Train up a child in the way he should go,
and when he is old he will not depart from it.

It is always our hope that our children will take what they've learned from us and carry it forward for the rest of their lives. But we also have to face the reality that they may not. I know plenty of Republicans whose parents are Democrats, and plenty of Democrats whose parents are Republicans. I know people who grew up supporting the sports teams their parents liked but have since switched allegiances. And while there are people who were not raised to believe in God who believe in Him today, there are also plenty of people who were raised to believe in God but no longer do.

I never lost my belief that there is a God, but I did not always have the passion for Him, the love for Him, the indebtedness toward Him that my mother and father had. It was not their fault. It was a choice I made as I grew up, capable of making my own decisions. They raised me to believe in Him, to worship Him, to love Him. I just chose a different path. But I eventually came back to the path they put me on, and without their help at that moment in time. I came back to it because they instilled high morals in me as I was growing up, and I knew what was right. They did their job, and it reflects in who I am today. It just took me some time to get there.

While our children are in our care, we need to put our hearts and souls into raising them with the highest moral standards possible. It is a responsibility we have not just toward them but toward the society in which they will live, the society in which they will raise their children, and in which their children will raise their children.

I said there is no manual on how to raise your children. But maybe the Bible is that manual. Even if you don't believe in God, or don't know where you stand regarding life after this one, take a look at the Bible—not as a religious book, but as a manual on how to live a good life. Share some of those instructions with your children, and I believe you'll have a difficult time going wrong as a parent.

Life stops for nobody

I mentioned earlier that while we were in the tower getting ready to leave that first time, I had wished I could have called a time-out.

If I just had a couple of minutes to get myself organized, to make sure that nothing influenced the decision I had made to leave, we all would have escaped. There used to be a television show in the 1960s and 1970s called *Bewitched,* where the witches could wave their hands and make everything and everyone around them freeze. The witches would then set things up the way they wanted, start the world up again, and life would continue. But that's Hollywood, not real life.

After the attacks, the stock markets closed for nearly a week, airspace over the city was temporarily shut down, and businesses went under. But life did not stop. People in other places in the city, country, and world went to work. Babies continued to be born. People still went on vacations, worked in the yard, got married. In fact, for some, the world went at an even faster pace—for the rescuers, the hospital workers, the news media, and the government, all of which had to instantly respond to the attacks.

For the families of the victims, life sadly continued with funeral arrangements, final good-byes, and trying to figure out how they were supposed to move forward hour by hour without their husbands, wives, fathers, mothers, children. When I was buried under the rubble, I would have given anything to be able to make the world stop as, with each passing second, death crept closer.

But what I learned from my experience is that if we accept the fact that life will never, ever stop for anybody, we can use it as motivation to make the most of the time we have, to live each day with a vigor that makes every moment count. As time continued to pass while I was under the debris, I finally started to use it wisely by getting closer and closer to God, and it led to my becoming the better person I am today. For those who lost loved ones in the attacks, hopefully life's refusal to stop has distanced them, even if just a tiny bit, from the pain they felt on 9/11. Hopefully it has brought them happiness in other ways—through new relationships, through service, or through political efforts to make the country a safer place for future generations.

I think realizing that life will continue no matter what, and no matter who you are, is half the battle toward living every day to the fullest. The rest of the battle is just living it in a positive light—by giving of yourself to others, working hard at everything you do, loving everybody around you, not fretting over the small stuff, appreciating what you have, not holding grudges, living your dreams, smiling a lot . . .

Robert Brault, a U.S. magazine and newspaper freelance writer for more than forty years, once wrote:

Why be saddled with this thing called life expectancy? Of what relevance to an individual is such a statistic? Am I to concern myself with an allotment of days I never had and was never promised? Must I check off each day of my life as if I am subtracting from this imaginary hoard? No, on the contrary, I will add each day of my life to my treasure of days lived. And with each day, my treasure will grow, not diminish.

Life will not stop, and as it continues full steam ahead, death draws nearer. But why fret? As long as we make the most of every moment of each day, and live the right way, it doesn't matter how fast it's going. It doesn't matter, as Brault points out, what our allotment of days is. We don't have to look at each passing day as a day closer to death, but as another magnificent memory of life.

Lean on your friends and family, and be there for them

I think the term "friend" is so loosely tossed around today with the advancement of technology that sometimes people lose focus of what a true friend is—what it means to have one, and what it means to be one. Of the "friends" you have on social-networking sites, how many are really your friends in the sense that you would call upon them if you needed something? How many of them would call upon you? Of all the people you "follow" on social-networking sites, how many would you truly follow if they were standing right in front of you? I don't see anything wrong with social-networking sites. In fact, there is a lot of good that can come from them. But never mistake them for what true friendships are.

George Eliot, a nineteenth-century novelist, once said:

Friendship is the inexpressible comfort of feeling safe with a person, having neither to weigh thoughts nor measure words.

That was Rosa and me. We could say anything to each other at any time. Our relationship didn't have much time behind it—I hadn't known her for more than seven or eight months—but we clicked from day one and quickly grew to be good friends. And if there was any thought that what we had was nothing more than a social relationship, that was quashed on 9/11 when we supported each other, emotionally and physically, from beginning to end. I think the most poignant sign of our friendship was when I started crying just before we went down the stairs and she soothingly squeezed my hand. Up to that point, I had probably been her pillar of support a little more than she had been mine. But through all the trouble she was having dealing with the situation, she came through for me when I needed it most, without uttering a single word—just a simple squeeze of my hand. When two people can communicate so simply, yet so powerfully, you know they share an indestructible bond.

Another quote about friendship that I can easily relate to my life is from Mark Twain, who said:

> The proper office of a friend is to side with you when you are in the wrong. Nearly anybody will side with you when you are in the right.

Not too many people would have the nerve to stand next to a person who is covered in soot and injured from head to toe after being buried alive for twenty-seven hours and say, "Why didn't you get out when I told you to?" Only Roger, my best friend, could have gotten away with saying that to me. And his response to me in the days and weeks after 9/11 really defined, more than anything else, what a true friend is. He was at my side every day, helping me walk, reading the Bible to me, making sure I was getting the attention I needed from the hospital staff. Between work and being with me, his days were at least eighteen hours long, seven days a week for six straight weeks.

I sometimes imagine what it would have been like to have been pulled from that rubble but with nobody there for me afterward. What if I was an only child and without parents, children of my own, a husband or boyfriend, and any true friends? People all over the world suffer from loneliness on a daily basis. I think that, too often, many of us take the companionship we have for granted and just assume there will always be people there for us, or people who will call on us when they need help. What if Roger wasn't there for me? What if our families weren't there for him when he thought I was dead? What if Elvis wasn't there for Kimberly when she got the news? How would any of us have made it through something so traumatic on our own? There's just no way.

One of the truest, simplest passages I've ever read about friendship comes from the Bible, in Ecclesiastes 4:9–10. It says:

Two are better than one, because they have a good reward for their labor. For if they fall, one will lift up his companion. But woe to him who is alone when he falls, for he has no one to help him up.

Do not ever take friends for granted. Offer them advice when they seek it, lend an ear when they want to talk, hold their hand when they need comfort, lend your shoulder when they cry, enjoy their company, make sacrifices for them, and share your life with them. True friends will do the same for you. That's what friendship is.

Know what is important in life

I'm not going to tell people what should be important in their lives. They know what should be important to them. I do not. We all have different priorities. Mine are God, then family, then work. Someone else may have the same three at the top, but in a different order. But just know what your priorities should be, and don't get distracted from keeping them in place.

I keep my priorities in order by saying a prayer every morning when I wake up, thanking God for another day and asking Him to bless my family, my friends, and me. It's a quick prayer, but one that gets me focused on the day right from the start. I then concentrate on my husband and children as we get ready for work, school, or whatever it is we're doing that day. From there, I focus on my work to help support my family and provide the basic necessities for living.

I think when I was born in 1971, priorities were much simpler to maintain. The world was less populated, the media wasn't as prevalent, technology did not enable one side of the world to communicate with the other side as cheaply and efficiently as it does today. Kids would go to school, dads and moms would go to work, evenings were spent watching one of just a few television stations available, and that was about it. Dinner was generally eaten at home together, as fast-food restaurants were few and far between. Playing generally meant doing something outside or at a friend's house. Sounds boring, but it wasn't. It was just different. It was the way life was back then. There was less of everything, and I think it helped people keep their lives under a little bit more control.

Today, the distractions are endless. I know adults who get

so hooked on video games, that they spend more time on them than they spend with their children or spouses. I've heard of people spending more time at work addressing personal emails or chatting on the Internet than they do on their jobs. And the infatuation many people have with celebrities and athletes is unprecedented.

I'm a great example of someone who used to have her priorities out of whack. When I was a child, listening to Michael Jackson's latest hits was much higher on my priority list than listening to God. As I grew up, spending time out on the town was more important than spending time with my family. How I looked on the outside was more important to me than who I was on the inside.

There is nothing wrong with having fun or even having interest in trivial matters. I do myself. But I've learned that problems can set in when those types of things inch up higher and higher on the priority list, knocking down those matters that should be more important. "To each his own" is an old saying in which I believe. But hopefully people can learn from my mistakes and understand that if they lose sight of what their priorities should be, the consequences could be devastating.

Make good come from bad

I believe something good can always come from something bad, even when that something bad is death. That doesn't mean that the pain the deceased's loved ones feel goes away. It doesn't, ever. But maybe it can soften a little bit by their finding a silver lining.

Deadly car crashes over the years have resulted in successful campaigns to create safer cars, which have probably saved thousands upon thousands of lives. Fires in buildings that took lives in the past have produced strict standards when buildings are constructed today, such as emergency exits and sprinkler systems, which have undoubtedly saved lives. The AMBER Alert system was named for a nine-year-old girl in Texas named Amber Hagerman who was abducted and murdered in 1996. The system has likely prevented many child abductions, and versions of it have been implemented in countries around the world.

The attacks on our country on 9/11 brought Americans together like nothing ever seen in my lifetime. Before then, I remember days like Veterans Day being little more than just another day on the calendar. Now everybody properly honors veterans on that day, including school children nationwide, who welcome veterans into their schools and hold special celebrations for them.

Several foundations and other money-raising efforts resulted from 9/11. One example is the Kenny & Brian Williams Fund. The Williams family, from Kentucky, tragically lost two sons. Kenny fell from a skywalk in downtown Cincinnati and spent three years in a coma until he died in 1994. Brian worked for Cantor Fitzgerald in the same building I was in, but about forty floors above me. As a result of the brothers' deaths, their friends and family started the fund to provide high school and college scholarships and to help families that are dealing with tragic events. In 2010, they held their last fundraiser. Why? Because they raised enough money in nine years for the fund to become self-sustaining. So because those two men died, people across the country have been helped, and will forever be helped, by the fund. The pain felt by the brothers' parents will never subside, but there has to be some joy in their hearts, knowing that the legacy of their sons will be helping others for years to come.

My life will forever be an example of good coming from bad. What I went through on 9/11 is something I would not wish upon anybody. The tragic loss of my friends and coworkers will forever leave an emptiness in my heart. The brutal memories of the building collapsing and burying me alive will never go away. But what happened that day changed my life forever in a good way too. It made me realize that the rest of my life needed to be lived differently. I needed to grow up, change my ways, and become the good person my parents raised me to be. Not only have I done that, but now I've shared my story through this book with the hope that others will be touched by my transformation and will be able to turn their lives around.

Bad things are going to happen here on earth. That will never change. People will die tragically, violence will persist, crimes will be committed, jobs will be lost, people will argue. These are all parts of life. But something good can always come from something bad. It usually just takes a little effort, a little time, a little hope, a little faith.

Everything happens for a reason

This may sound familiar to you:

> *To everything there is a season, a time for every purpose under heaven:*

A time to be born, and a time to die; a time to plant, and a
    time to pluck what is planted;
A time to kill, and a time to heal; a time to break down, and
    a time to build up;
A time to weep, and a time to laugh; a time to mourn, and a
    time to dance;
A time to cast away stones, and a time to gather stones; a
    time to embrace, and a time to refrain from embracing;
A time to gain, and a time to lose; a time to keep, and a time
    to throw away;
A time to tear, and a time to sew; a time to keep silence, and
    a time to speak;
A time to love, and a time to hate; a time of war, and a time
    of peace.

Many people will recognize it as being very similar to the lyrics of the 1965 number one song "Turn! Turn! Turn!" by the Byrds. But it is actually from the book of Ecclesiastes 3:1–8, from which the song was adapted. Many people believe that first line, "To everything there is a season, a time for every purpose under heaven," is the biblical proof that everything happens for a reason.

How often have you heard that phrase—everything happens for a reason? Probably many times, especially in difficult situations. It's a tough phrase for some people to accept because it basically means that everything, good and bad, can happen beyond their control. But isn't every aspect of life, in some way, beyond our control? Look at the two most significant times of our lives, and the second line of that passage—our birth and our death. We don't control either one. We are born when God decides we will be born. When we will die is also a mystery to each of us. And while we may feel that we have some control of our destinies between life and death, I don't think we have nearly as much as we think we do.

Take a look at my day on September 11, 2001. I slept well and woke up in a great mood, thanks primarily to making up with Roger a couple of days earlier after a two-week argument. I caught the 7 a.m. train into town, walked the rest of the way into work, turned on my computer, got breakfast, went back to my desk, felt the building shake, spent the next ninety or so minutes trying to figure out what to do, finally made my way down the stairs, and got caught in the midst of the building's collapse.

It would appear, on the surface, that I was pretty much in control of everything. I decided when to wake up, how to get to work, when to leave for work, to go get breakfast after turning on my computer, to not leave the building after it was hit, to eventually go down the stairs. But was that all really the case?

I woke up in a great mood that morning because Roger and I were back together. Had we not made up, I would have been back at my niece's house, where I had been living for the previous two weeks, which would have altered my course to work that morning and possibly gotten me into work later. But go back further. I wouldn't have fought with Roger if I didn't know him in the first place, and the only reason I knew him was because he happened to spot me at a carnival in another country among thousands of people. What if I had walked in a different direction five seconds before he spotted me? He never would have even seen me, which means we never would have met, which means the chain of events that followed would have altered both of our lives forever. I could go back even further and say that if I never decided to move to New York in the first place . . .

As another example, what if I had missed the 7 a.m. train and showed up a little later for work? What if, as a result of showing up later, I was still in the forty-fourth-floor cafeteria when the plane hit? Would I have gone back up to my desk, or just gotten out of the building? My decision probably would have been determined based on what other people there were doing. And if I had gotten out, I wouldn't have been buried alive. And if I hadn't been buried alive, I probably would be drinking at a bar right now like my old self instead of writing my memoir.

Look at someone like James Symington. If he wasn't where he was with Trakr, searching for live victims, Trakr would have never picked up my scent. If he hadn't picked up my scent, rescuers such as Rick Cushman and others may not have been looking as closely as they were for victims in that area of the rubble. Then I wouldn't have been found. Or maybe I would have, because Paul did say that somebody was coming. But if I hadn't found God under that rubble, would Paul have even shown up? Then Roger's and Kimberly's lives would have been affected forever. Roger and I wouldn't have married. The two children we had together would never have been born. It's likely Kimberly would have never come to America. And it goes on and on and on.

Every moment of our lives comes from something that happened, or didn't happen, previously. Why are you reading this book now? Maybe because the bookstore had it, you bought it, and you went straight home to read it. What if that store didn't have it in stock and you decided to go to another store, but on your way to that store, you were in a car accident? And maybe that initial store didn't have the book because a shipment didn't get out in time from a warehouse on the other side of the country . . . because some guy called in sick and the staff was shorthanded. Had that guy not called in sick, is it conceivable to say that you would not have gotten in that accident? Every moment happens for a reason, a reason beyond our control. A reason that is part of God's master plan for our lives.

I've heard the question before, "Why pray if God has a plan for us?" It's a valid question. If God gives us life with a plan in place, what is the point in praying if our destiny has been predetermined? I'm not a religious scholar, and I'm not going to try to be, but I think one reason prayer is necessary is that Satan lives to hinder God's plans. I think prayer strengthens our relationship with God, shows Him we care about the plan He has for us, and helps us stay on course with that plan. I think God had a plan for me to be His servant for life, but I followed the devil's ways and strayed from Him. Once I began to pray, and pray hard, while buried alive, I believe it put me back on the course He had originally designed for me when He brought me into this world. Now He trusts that I will stay on that course until He decides to take me out of this world.

One of my favorite proverbs that relates to this lesson is from Proverbs 3:5–6, which says: *Trust in the LORD with all your heart, and lean not on your own understanding; in all your ways acknowledge Him, and He shall direct your paths.*

"Trust in the LORD with all your heart." How many of us do that all the time? It's an enormous challenge every day. It goes back to that control issue. We all want control in everything we do, but we need to trust that no matter how much we worry or stress over something, it's all going to work out the way God wants it to. Whatever happens will happen for a reason.

"Lean not on your own understanding." Another aspect of human nature is to trust our own judgment first. God gave us brains, and many of us have a tendency to use those brains to think we're smarter than Him or that we know what's better for us than He does. Too often we try to rationalize situations based on what we think is right, rather than what God thinks is right, which is clearly spelled out in the Bible. I know people who break the commandment of keeping holy the Sabbath day and try to justify it by saying they have to work, sleep, or recover from their hangovers. That used to be me. I know people who don't keep the commandment of not taking the Lord's name in vain and don't think it's a big deal. Others don't think twice about bearing false witness against their neighbors—me again, years ago. Do not trust your own understanding. Trust God's understanding. Follow the Bible, His instruction manual for how to live.

"In all your ways acknowledge Him, and He shall direct your paths." If we consistently keep Him at the forefront of our minds in everything we do, He will lead us up a path of goodness, which ends in His kingdom.

By believing that everything happens for a reason, we're acknowledging that God is greater than we are, knows better than we, and is watching over us all the time. It means we believe that for everything there is a season, a time for every purpose under heaven. Take it from the Bible, or from the Byrds. In either case, it's a great lesson.

CHAPTER TWENTY-FOUR

The Terrorists

In the days and weeks after 9/11 when I started watching the news and trying to figure out what happened, I kept hearing the name Osama bin Laden and didn't have a clue who he was. Reporters were referring to him as the leader of the terrorist group al-Qaeda, an Islamic extremist disowned by his wealthy Saudi Arabian family and believed to be hiding in the rugged mountains near Afghanistan. It was surreal to me that one man living in one of the most remote parts of the world could have such influence over people that he could convince them to fly airplanes into New York City and Washington, DC, buildings. But he did.

As the years went on and I still hadn't really been able to figure out why bin Laden did what he did other than the fact that he was pure evil and was out to destroy American lives for his own sick satisfaction, I read a quote that was attributed to him in 2004 that I was hoping would help me better understand his reasoning:

Allah knows it did not cross our minds to attack the towers but after the situation became unbearable and we witnessed the injustice and tyranny of the American-Israeli alliance against our people in Palestine and Lebanon, I thought about it. And the events that affected me directly were that of 1982 and the events that followed—when America allowed the Israelis to invade Lebanon, helped by the U.S. Sixth Fleet . . . As I watched the destroyed towers in Lebanon, it occurred to me to punish the unjust the same way (and) to destroy towers in America so it could taste some of what we are tasting and to stop killing our children and women.

Well, that didn't help me a whole lot. I honestly don't follow politics closely enough to understand all of the United States' alliances and relations with foreign countries and certainly didn't follow what happened in 1982, when I was just eleven and living in Trinidad. But what I did get from that, simply put, is that he sought revenge on the United States for what he felt were injustices committed against his people years earlier. So I and thousands of others were the innocent victims of one man's misplaced rage. I attempted to break down his comments to try the nearly impossible task of figuring out how he thinks, and I found the first thirteen words very intriguing:

"Allah knows it did not cross our minds to attack the towers but . . ."

It seems to me that by feeling the need to say that Allah knows they had no intention of attacking the towers, he's saying that Allah would not have approved of attacking them, "but . . ."

After that conjunction, everything he says falls into one of the lessons I learned about not leaning on your own understanding. That's exactly what he did. "Even though Allah would not approve of my destroying the towers, I will do so anyway because of the way *I* view the situation," is basically what I believe he was suggesting. What is even more amazing to me than his argument for killing so many innocent people is that he found nineteen men to buy into his cause. And they were so entrenched in his plan that they were willing to go through years of training, knowing that the end result was going to include not only killing innocent people but taking their own lives as well.

A question I have often been asked by the media and general public over the years is whether or not I have forgiven bin Laden and the other terrorists for what they did. It's an interesting question to which I'm not sure I can give a definitive yes or no answer.

I know that some people cannot move forward with their lives until they find a way to forgive someone who has wronged them, which is perfectly understandable. It's a form of closure for them, a way to try and bring themselves some peace. But somehow I have been able to move forward without the need to even address that question within my own heart. I guess if pressed to answer, I would say that, yes, I probably have forgiven them, simply because I have never let their actions control my life after 9/11. Yes, they hurt me deeply in so many ways, including killing my coworkers and my friend Rosa. But that time buried alive helped me to progress to such a peaceful place in my life that I never felt any hatred toward anybody. They made me very sad—sad beyond description—but not angry.

So I never felt the need to address the issue. Forgiveness is about making peace with yourself in your own heart, with God, and with the ones you are forgiving. I've been at peace with myself and with God, and I know bin Laden and the terrorists, before they died, couldn't have cared less whether I made peace with them.

God was with me when the towers fell, and He is with me now. And that is all that matters.

EPILOGUE

Since I finished my rehabilitation in 2003, I have been in very good health. My heart is beating like a heart should. There have been no signs of cancer since the treatment I received in 2001. I walk with a slight limp, so slight that many people normally don't notice. But considering doctors thought there was a chance I wouldn't even have a right leg to limp on, I'm certainly not going to complain.

I haven't had any marked emotional "issues" over the years as a result of being buried alive. I mean it when I say that God was my psychiatrist, and still is today. I've been blessed by never having a single nightmare about my experience. Not a day goes by that I don't think of Rosa, Susan, or any of the others who lost their lives, but it doesn't haunt me. Instead, I say a little prayer and smile with the comfort of knowing they are with God, and that I will one day be reunited with them.

I never had a formal face-to-face reunion with Pasquale, the only other person in our group to survive, but we did talk on the phone once we both returned to work. We caught up with each other on how we were doing physically and had plenty to talk about regarding our new families. While I got married in November 2001, his wife gave birth to their daughter that same month. We talked about those who died and shared our stories of what we remember happening that morning.

I've been asked many times over the years the same question that Roger asked when he first saw me in the hospital: why didn't we get out sooner? When I see pictures or video of the raging fire with desperate people hanging out windows or jumping to their deaths, I think *My God, Genelle, what were you thinking by staying there?* But it's all Monday-morning quarterbacking. I had no idea any of that was happening. It was a confusing situation from the get-go, one that I pray nobody ever has to experience again.

When thinking about those who jumped to their deaths, I've always held, and always will hold, a special place in my heart for them. I cannot get it out of my mind, after all of these years, what it must have been like for them to be forced to make that choice. But I don't believe they took their own lives. It wasn't suicide. Their lives had already been taken by the terrorists, whose actions gave them only two options: burn to death, or jump. I have no doubt that as quickly as they fell to the ground, their souls were lifted by God to heaven.

Talking about what happened that day has oddly never been difficult for me, but one thing I do each year is take September 11 off from work. The only time I did not take the day off was in 2006, and I wish I had. It was the fifth anniversary, and I really didn't know how I would react, or how others would react toward me being at work. It turned out to be a day of people constantly stopping by my desk to tell me they were thinking about me and that they were happy I survived. And while that was very kind of them, it was awkward for me and mentally tough to deal with for those eight long hours.

It's a day that I want to stay home, with the television off, or be in a church, praying, or doing something that gives me the comfort and freedom to concentrate and reflect on what happened that day. It's a day I like to both mourn and celebrate. Even to be happy. Despite the odds, I'm alive. Celebration and mourning are a complicated mix of emotions, but they're mine, and every year, on 9/11, I give myself the space to feel them.

As for Ground Zero, I've been there a couple of times since 9/11. It doesn't bother me to go back, because it has changed so much. I'm very appreciative that a memorial has been built there. Nobody who is old enough to remember what happened will ever forget, and the memorial gives them a significant place to pay their respects. And for those too young to remember what happened, it gives them a place—*the* place—to learn about one of the most significant events in our nation's history.

Of course, the most significant result of my time buried under the tower is my relationship with God. It is one of the greatest gifts I've ever been given, and although it happened in the most terrible circumstance, I am always eager to tell my story. People can debate whether or not Paul was an angel. They can argue whether or not it was coincidence that I was found beneath the rubble after I started praying and calling out to God. People can question whether or not God even exists, and if I just happened to be lucky. All I can say is that, from my perspective, something dramatic happened to me after the attacks. While I was buried alive, I know what I saw, I know what I heard, I know what I felt, and it all radically changed my life forever. If you had known me before 9/11, you would not believe that I am the person I am today.

There is hope for everybody. No matter how bad your life may seem, how deep your troubles are, or how much you've drifted away from what you believe is right and good, you always have the ability to change.

Sometimes I wonder what would have happened if I had left the building sooner and escaped unharmed. I bet I would have been grateful to be out but would have given credit to myself for deciding to leave when I did, or given credit to myself for taking off my shoes when I did so that I could move faster, or . . . me, me, me, me, me. It would have been all about me before I would have ever considered giving God any credit at all. And I'm absolutely certain I would have chalked it up to being lucky and would have continued living the same old life I was living. That God saved me, for whatever reason, brings me great joy and hope for the future. I think of Jesus' parable from Scripture:

> *What man of you, having a hundred sheep, if he loses one of them, does not leave the ninety-nine in the wilderness, and go after the one which is lost until he finds it? And when he has found it, he lays it on his shoulders, rejoicing. And when he comes home, he calls together his friends and neighbors, saying to them, "Rejoice with me, for I have found my sheep which was lost!"*

I say to you that likewise there will be more joy in heaven over one sinner who repents than over ninety-nine just persons who need no repentance. (Luke 15:4–7)

My life, and my choices, have been far from perfect since that day. But I do strive to be better, to be loving, to be a light for God through my thoughts, my words, and my actions—as a wife, mother, friend, coworker and even stranger. At my best, I can offer my hand to those who need it, just as Paul offered his to me. It is the least I can do.

ACKNOWLEDGMENTS

This book has two names on the cover, but it took the creative ideas, invaluable critiques, and unconditional support from countless people over many months for it to come to fruition.

A special thank you to our agent, Ronald Goldfarb, who not only found a good home for our work, but whose very first question of, "What can people learn from this book?" helped guide us to craft this project around the answer: "There is always hope."

Thank you to Roger McMillan and Kimberly YipYing, who provided their unique perspectives of September 11 and the aftermath in tremendous detail and supported us throughout this venture. And to Gary Tuchman, whose coverage and memories of 9/11 the day of and in the years following helped us recall history and tie it to today.

There were thousands of heroes on that tragic day, two of them being Rick Cushman and James Symington. They put their lives on hold to travel hundreds of miles in search of total strangers simply because their good hearts told them that's what they should do. We will be forever grateful to you for your valor and for vividly recounting your stories to us.

Thank you to Nicci Jordan Hubert, the first official editor of the manuscript. Her enthusiasm and talent helped mold this book into what it is today.

Philis Boultinghouse, Susan Wilson, Jennifer Smith, Bruce Gore, and many others behind the scenes at Howard Books and Simon & Schuster edited, designed, produced, and publicized the book. Your expertise shines through this work. Thank you for all you did, all you continue to do, and your confidence in us every step of the way.

While crafting the first draft, we asked five avid readers with various backgrounds to assess our work and help guide us toward the finish line. Thank you to Debra Croyle, Anne Pillai, Judy Jakyma, Chrissie Parente, and Lisa Kovach. Your contributions were immeasurable.

To Phyllis Mazzella, whose battle with cancer and pursuit of hope the past two years was an inspiration every day during the writing of this book.

Finally, the support necessary in writing a book comes in several forms, including emotional. There were literally hundreds of family members and friends who encouraged us throughout this long journey. Your continual optimism and vision for what this book could become and the positive effect it could have on the lives of people around the world kept us on track and helped us reach our destination. Thank you.